MOON METRO
SAN FRANCISCO

CONTENTS

AVALON TRAVEL

HOW TO USE THIS BOOK

MAP SECTION

- We've divided San Francisco into eight distinct areas. Each area has been assigned a color, used on the map itself and in easy-to-spot map number indicators throughout the listings.

- The maps show the location of every listing in the book, using the icon that indicates what type of listing it is (sight, restaurant, etc.) and the listing's locator number.

- The coordinates (in color) indicate the specific grid that the listing is located in. The black number is the listing's locator number. The page number directs you to the listing's full description.

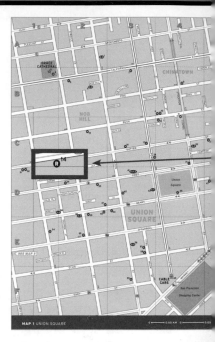

MAP 1 UNION SQUARE

LISTINGS SECTION

- Listings are organized into six sections:

  ○ SIGHTS

  ○ RESTAURANTS

  ○ NIGHTLIFE

  ○ SHOPS

  ○ ARTS AND LEISURE

  ○ HOTELS

- Within each section, listings are organized by which map they are located in, then in alphabetical order.

MAP 1 UNION SQUARE

ANZU *BUSINESS • SUSHI/STEAK $$$*
The refined, tranquil Anzu takes the concept of yin and yang into uncharted territory. Not only do the sushi creations rival those of the best Japanese restaurants, they make a delightful complement to the menu's other specialty, prime aged steaks from Allen Brothers of Chicago.
MAP 1 E3 ○ 56   222 MASON ST. (HOTEL NIKKO)   415-394-1100

B44 *BUSINESS • CATALAN $$*
At lunchtime, this Catalan bistro is crammed with suits, seated in the chic dining room or outside on an alley lined with European cafés. Come dinner, the noise subsides. Choose a rioja to go with one of the eight paella options.
MAP 1 B6 ○ 12   44 BELDEN PL.   415-986-6287

CAFÉ CLAUDE *CAFÉ • FRENCH $*
With a wait staff imported directly from France, this charming bistro is a Parisian delight. Live jazz and an extensive wine list perfectly complement the delicately succulent menu, which includes soupe à l'oignon gratinée, baguette avec brie, and quiche aux legumes.
MAP 1 C5 ○ 23   7 CLAUDE LN.   415-392-3515

CAMPTON PLACE *ROMANTIC • CALIFORNIA-MEDITERRANEAN $$$*
Presentation is key for 20-something chef Daniel Humm, who creates works of art with dishes like wild Mediterranean branzino (sea bass) and zucchini-wrapped squab. The elegant dining room, complete with deep plush booths, provides the perfect spot to appreciate his masterpieces.
MAP 1 C4 ○ 20   340 STOCKTON ST. (CAMPTON PLACE HOTEL)   415-955-5555

CORTEZ *HOT SPOT • MEDITERRANEAN $$*
San Francisco restaurateur extraordinaire Pascal Rigo has elevated the casual hotel restaurant to new levels with his latest venture. Date- and mint-crusted lamb, plump crab cakes, and shoestring fries with zippy Moroccan dips pair with creative cocktails in this loft-like comfortable space.
MAP 1 D2 ○ 36   550 GEARY ST. (HOTEL ADAGIO)   415-292-6360

DOTTIE'S TRUE BLUE CAFÉ *BREAKFAST AND BRUNCH • AMERICAN $*
This classic Tenderloin joint garners adoration and acclaim from its devotees by doling out massive three-egg omelets, fat slices of French toast, homemade breads, and cinnamon-swirled streusel coffeecake. Stuff yourself silly.
MAP 1 E1 ○ 54   522 JONES ST.   415-885-2767

1. Scan the map to see what listings are in the area you want to explore. Use the directory to find out the name and page number for each listing.

2. Read the listings to find the specific place you want to visit. Use the map information at the bottom of each listing to find the listing's exact location.

MAP KEY

Major Sight	★
BART Station	🅱
Bus Line	—Ⓝ—
Cable Car Line	o—O
Shopping District	———
Stairs	‖‖‖‖‖‖
Pedestrian Street	———
Adjacent Map Boundaries	SEE MAP 1 ▷

SECTION ICONS

Ⓢ SIGHTS

Ⓡ RESTAURANTS

Ⓝ NIGHTLIFE

Ⓢ SHOPS

Ⓐ ARTS AND LEISURE

Ⓗ HOTELS

RESTAURANTS

GRAND CAFÉ

'ARALLON ...
his temple of ...
uuah, aiu ur ...
ool. Each is a ...
ially menu – ...
ent raw bar.
D3 41

IRST CRUSH ...
n vintner's ter ...
of the harvest ...
ourse prix fixe ...
ard-colored di ...
he California ...
E3 58

FLEUR DE LY ...
amous for its ...
he site of wed ...
ears. Esteemer ...
rench fare in t ...
egetarian mer ...
C1Ⓡ14 777 SUTTER ST.
415-673-7779

GRAND CAFÉ ROMANTIC • CALIFORNIA-FRENCH $$$
The Hotel Monaco's majestic ballroom-cum-art gallery – complete with early-20th-century murals, trompe l'oeil, and modern sculpture – provides the backdrop for celebratory California-French feasting. Start with the duck confit, and move on to roasted rack of lamb or sautéed skate wing.
D2Ⓡ38 501 POST ST.
415-292-0101

HANA ZEN BUSINESS • JAPANESE $$
This sleek and stylish restaurant offers one of the most engaging extensive Japanese menus in town, including one sparkling rarity: authentic yakitori, or grilled fowl. À la carte standouts include a

FLEUR DE LYS ROMANTIC • FRENCH $$$
Famous for its mammoth garden-tent venue, Fleur de Lys has been the site of wedding proposals and celebrations for more than 30 years. Esteemed chef Hubert Keller creates bold and beautiful French fare in three-, four-, and five-course spreads. Tasting and vegetarian menus are also available.

MAP 1 C1Ⓡ14 777 SUTTER ST.
415-673-7779

Use the **MAP NUMBER, COLOR GRID COORDINATES**, and **BLACK LOCATOR NUMBER** to find the exact location of every listing in the book.

INTRODUCTION TO
SAN FRANCISCO

When engineers laid out the streets of San Francisco, they modeled the city after board-flat urban centers in America's Midwest. They may as well have tried to fit a siren into a schoolgirl's uniform. The regular grid pattern found on maps leaves visitors unprepared for the precipitous inclines and stunning water views in this town built on 43 hills.

Geographically and culturally, San Francisco is anything but flat, and what level ground exists might at any moment give way. While earthquakes remake the land, social upheavals play a similar role in reminding that the only constant here is change. In the 1950s, the Beats challenged postwar conformity and left a legacy of incantatory poems and independent bookstores. The late 1960s saw a years-long Summer of Love, which shifted consciousness as surely as quakes shift tectonic plates. During the same period, the Black Panther party was founded across the bay in Oakland, and other ethnic and cultural groups were redefining their identities against mainstream America. Gay and lesbian liberation movements sprung forth in the 1970s, as did a renewed push for women's rights. More recently, the dot-com and tech booms added their frantic energy to the mix.

Surrounded by water on three sides, San Francisco is a city of microclimates. Sweatered residents of the Richmond district may be huddled in cafes to escape the fog, while friends in the Mission sit on their stoops in shirtsleeves, soaking up the sun. Visitors may be surprised by thick fog in July and August, or with the warmest day of the year coming in early October.

IT WAS A DARK AND FOGGY NIGHT

No city is more film noir than San Francisco. From the Humphrey Bogart masterpiece, *The Maltese Falcon* (1941) to lesser-known pictures, such as *Shakedown* (1950) and *The Sniper* (1951), movies have repeatedly featured San Francisco and its foggy city nights – when the narrow alleys are chilly and dark and the side streets are damp and slippery – to set a mood of forlorn menace. Consider *Dark Passage* (1947) with its murder under the Golden Gate Bridge or *Experiment in Terror* (1962) with its tense climax at Candlestick Park. However, the quintessential San Francisco crime picture remains Alfred Hitchcock's *Vertigo* (1958). Co-written by a native San Franciscan, the film uses the city almost like a character, tracing the hills, coastline, Victorians, and streets in almost gratuitous detail. This classic's eerie tour of municipal landmarks includes Nob Hill, Mission Dolores, the Palace of the Legion of Honor, and Fort Point. To get a feel for San Francisco's noir side, follow the spirit of Madeleine Elster (played by Kim Novak in *Vertigo*), and "walk all the hills, explore the edge of the ocean, see all the old houses, and wander the old streets."

Though San Francisco is the most-visited city in the United States, it often seems like a provincial village, or a series of villages that share a downtown and a roster of world-class icons. Drive over the Golden Gate or the Bay Bridge as the fog is lifting, and your heart will catch at the ever-changing beauty of the scene. Stand at the base of the Transamerica Pyramid, hang off the side of a cable car, or just walk through the neighborhoods that make the city more than the sum of its parts. Despite the hills, San Francisco is a city that cries out to be explored on foot.

The fog rolls in and out; the city reels and rights itself through earthquakes and boom-and-bust cycles. For all its mutability and contrariness, San Francisco has staying power. In the realm of the imagination, it easily displaces bigger cities with more impressive credentials. Willfully young and a little raw, San Francisco nevertheless has a talent for living its moment fully – from Gold Rush to Flower Power to dot-com to whatever comes next. New arrivals – visitors and residents both – come to live the eternal present of the city that captivates even as it shifts underfoot.

HISTORY

Waves of immigration have played their part in defining San Francisco. The area's original inhabitants were Ohlone Indians, who shared the peninsula with grizzly bears, herds of elk, and flocks of geese so dense they darkened the sky. The Ohlone got a reprieve when, in 1579, Sir Frances Drake sailed right past the opening to San Francisco Bay. Other explorers missed it, too; it wasn't until almost two centuries later that the first Europeans sailed through the Golden Gate.

QUEER SAN FRANCISCO

With one of the largest annual Lesbian/Gay/Bisexual/Transgender (LGBT) pride parades in the world and a queer community that makes up an estimated 25–30 percent of the city's population, it's no wonder San Francisco is considered one of the world's most famous "gay meccas." Queer culture has played a significant part in defining the city for decades.

In 1964, *Life* magazine declared San Francisco "the gay capital of the United States," due in part to the fact that two of the leading national gay organizations – the Mattachine Society and the Daughters of Bilitis (the first national lesbian organization) – had been headquartered in San Francisco since the 1950s. The 1977 election of gay activist Harvey Milk to the San Francisco Board of Supervisors brought recognition of the gay rights movement to a new level. At that time, the Castro district began to flourish as the city's gay neighborhood and it eventually became the epicenter of the queer community. Although the community was hit hard by the murder of Milk and the AIDS epidemic in the 1980s and early 1990s, queer life in the city continued, extending beyond the Castro district to most parts of the city (the Mission district is a popular scene for lesbians). More recently, in February 2004, the LGBT movement received national attention when Mayor Gavin Newsom asked the county clerk to create "non-discriminatory" marriage license forms. Today, much of the city's queer history is preserved at **The Center (p. 82),** and the four-hour **Cruisin' the Castro Walking Tour (p. 88)** traces the origins of the queer community, pointing out various historical landmarks along the way.

The aboriginal culture went into quick decline with the arrival of the Spanish, who founded the city in 1776, just as the United States declared independence from England. The first colonizing party built a *presidio* (fort) and founded the Mission Dolores (La Misión de San Francisco de Asis), then came a village called Yerba Buena, a name that stuck until the city became San Francisco in 1847. A year later gold was discovered, and soon more than 100,000 '49ers (named for the year they arrived) flooded in to make their fortune. Chinese began arriving in large numbers during this time, too – that year San Francisco's population shot from 500

to 25,000. The 20th century saw successive waves of newcomers – from beatniks to dotcommers, from immigrants to gays. More recently, immigrants from other Asian countries, the Philippines, Russia, and South and Central America have added to the city's diversity.

OVER HILL AND DALE

In this city of mild weather and magnificent views, you should try to walk or take public transit whenever possible, but cable cars ascend only a few select hills, bus lines are slow and crowded, and cabs are expensive and scarce. That leaves the much-maligned automobile, but make sure your rental car is an automatic. Driving in this city with a standard transmission is an extreme sport. You may want to steer clear of the worst streets – the steepest is Filbert between Leavenworth and Hyde, with a 31.5 percent grade. The only thing worse than driving these grades is trying to park on them. Bank your wheels toward the curb if you're pointed downhill and toward the street if you're faced uphill.

UNION SQUARE **CABLE CAR** **CITY LIGHTS**

THE BEST OF
SAN FRANCISCO

San Francisco may only be roughly seven miles long and seven miles wide, but it packs in historic neighborhoods, one of the West Coast's most iconic landmarks, and dozens of stomach-dropping inclines within its small area. Exploring all its hills and alleys will take more than 24 hours, but it is possible to hit the essentials in one day. Of course, the Golden Gate Bridge is a must on any roundup of San Francisco's best, but you'll also want to see North Beach and take the cable car. Even touristy Fisherman's Wharf is a necessary stop in this city by the bay. Here's one way to do it — and all without wearing down your soles walking up the many steep slopes.

1 Start your day with a drive to the **Golden Gate Bridge (p. 19).** The span is beautiful at all times of day and year — and even in the city's notorious fog.

2 Drive back toward downtown, and ditch your car. Have breakfast at **Dottie's True Blue Cafe (p. 22).** Don't let the slightly gritty area turn you off — this is a local favorite.

3 From Dottie's, **Union Square (p. 56),** and its many surrounding shops, is only a few blocks. Walk off your breakfast while window-shopping the upscale boutiques.

4 Make your way to the foot of Powell Street at Market, and board the **cable car (p. 2).** Take the Powell-Hyde line, and ride it to the end. Watch for gorgeous bay views as the cable car crests Russian Hill around Filbert Street.

5 At the end of the line, you're just across the street from the **Buena Vista Cafe (p. 48),** said to have introduced Irish coffee to the States.

6 Stroll along **Fisherman's Wharf (p. 9)** and the waterfront. For lunch, pick up a clam chowder in a bread bowl from one of the many sidewalk vendors.

7 Near Pier 39, buy tickets for the hour-long **Bay Cruise (p. 86).** From the water, the views of the skyline and the Golden Gate Bridge are spectacular.

8 After the cruise, take a cab or walk to North Beach, San Francisco's Little Italy and one of its historic literary neighborhoods. Be sure to stop in **City Lights Bookstore (p. 58),** the legendary Beat Generation bookstore.

9 Dine on Italian food at **Rose Pistola (p. 32).** Try to get a seat facing Columbus Avenue – the street bustle is a San Francisco sight in itself.

10 Catch a cab to the Intercontinental Mark Hopkins for drinks overlooking the city at the **Top of the Mark (p. 44).** With a menu of 100 martinis and a dress code, it's a swank place to end your day.

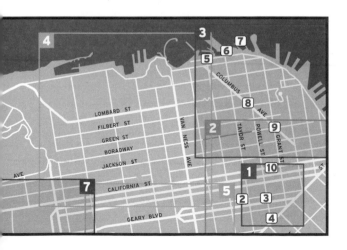

CITIZEN CAKE   BOULEVARD   BUBBLE LOUNGE

GOURMET
SAN FRANCISCO

With more restaurants per resident than any other U.S. city, San Francisco is very much an eating destination. The food attractions go well beyond wine and innovative California cuisine – although there's definitely plenty of that. San Franciscans take their food very seriously, and they're willing to go to all parts of the city to find the sweetest pastries and the stinkiest cheese. Take a day, and you can do it, too.

1 Grab breakfast pastries, like filled croissants and flaky buns, at **Citizen Cake (p. 35).** Despite its name, the Californian cuisine restaurant serves more than just dessert. On weekends, come for brunch.

2 Head to Hayes Street, where cute boutiques line both sides of the fashionable blocks between Franklin and Laguna. Foodies should make sure to stop in **Arlequin (p. 35)** for tasty snacks and adjoining **Amphora Wine Merchant (p. 62)** for well-priced wines.

3 From there, walk to Market Street, then down a couple blocks for lunch at **Zuni Cafe (p. 36).** This destination restaurant offers a changing Mediterranean-influenced menu.

4 After lunch, walk down to the Van Ness Muni station, and take the J Church outbound to 18th Street. The city's best bakery, **Tartine Bakery (p. 39),** is at Guerrero and 18th Streets. Everything's good, but if you have trouble choosing, you can't go wrong with the lemon meringues or the brownies.

⑤ Bring all your goodies to the slope at **Dolores Park (p. 88)** for a picnic of snacks overlooking the city. If you bought one earlier in the day, break out the bottle of wine to enjoy with your sweets.

⑥ Hop back on the J Church and take it all the way to Embarcadero station. Walk down to the **Ferry Building (p. 57)** where dozens of gourmet food stores – ranging from tea and ice cream to organic meats – will keep your mouth watering. If you need something else to snack on, try some aged cheese for a savory treat to balance the sweets.

⑦ Walk a couple blocks to **Boulevard (p. 26),** the dining room that often tops gourmet restaurant lists. Make reservations weeks in advance in order to guarantee a table, but a seat at the bar will also give you access to Nancy Oakes' award-winning California cuisine.

⑧ After dinner, take a cab to the plush **The Bubble Lounge (p. 29)** for champagne and a selection of exquisite desserts.

LOMBARD STREET   **ALAMO SQUARE**   **CONSERVATORY OF FLOWERS**

POSTCARD
SAN FRANCISCO

San Franciscans think their city is the most beautiful in the United States – and a competitor for the world title. With its hills, waterside location, and quirky Victorians, San Francisco is definitely easy on the eyes, but take a day and decide for yourself. Of course, a clear, sunny day is best for this excursion, but even in the famous fog, Lombard Street is still twisty and the Cliff House still gives up great front-row seats to the ocean. You'll need a car to hit all the sights, and at the end, you may have a hard time finding a postcard of something you *didn't* see.

1 Prepare for your full day with a hearty breakfast at **Ella's (p. 32),** one of San Francisco's favorite breakfast destinations.

2 From there, walk or drive to the top of the **Lyon Street Steps (p. 12),** where the view of the Palace of Fine Arts against the bay is breathtaking.

3 Jump back into your car so you can drive down **Lombard Street (p. 10).** Watch the cars before you (and there will probably be many) make their way gingerly down the brick-paved road, then slowly take your turn.

4 Turn toward the Western Addition for a stop at **Alamo Square (p. 13).** This is where you'll get the postcard view of the Seven Sisters, the most celebrated Painted Ladies in a city full of Victorian-style buildings. This is mainly a photo-op: these landmarks aren't open to the public.

5 For lunch, go to **Cha Cha Cha (p. 39)** on **Haight Street (p. 70)** for tapas. On the way to or from the restaurant, check out the hippie-era murals, used clothing stores, and record shops that line this famous street. Stop at the corner of Haight and Ashbury for a photo with the famous street sign.

6 From the Haight, Golden Gate Park is a quick walk. Make your way to the **Conservatory of Flowers (p. 17),** one of the prettiest spots (inside and out) in an all-around beautiful park.

7 Back in your car, get to the other side of the park and take Geary or Clement to the **Palace of the Legion of Honor (p. 18).** Rodin's *Thinker* sits in the entrance, and many of his other sculptures are on display inside. Afterward – or perhaps instead – stroll around the museum for perfect views of the Golden Gate Bridge.

8 From the museum, you're only a five-minute drive away from the **Cliff House (p. 41),** a restaurant that sits, as its name implies, on a seaside cliff. Sunsets are a great event here.

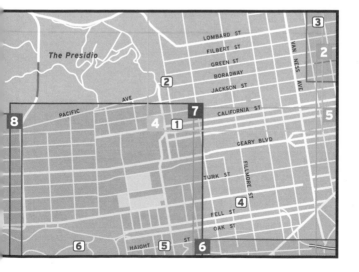

UNION SQUARE

Within the oft-debated confines of downtown, Union Square is San Francisco's main shopping district and the dynamic heart of the city. Named for a series of mass demonstrations in support of Union troops that took place here on the eve of the Civil War, the area bears little resemblance to its appearance in the early days. During Gold Rush times, downtown was a raucous, vice-filled zone, with 10 men to every woman, and the streets were lined with saloons, gambling halls, and brothels.

Today in Union Square, the money still flows freely, but within more staid channels. Lined with high-end department stores and designer showrooms, the plaza and the streets around it are also home to some of the city's most opulent hotels and stylish restaurants. The Square itself recently emerged from a $25 million renovation, with new landscaping, sculptures, a large central plaza with a terraced performance stage, lawn seating, and a café with outdoor seating. Side streets yield up art galleries, private clubs, and luxurious salons. Catch one of the cable cars that run along Powell Street and ride up to Nob Hill, where the gothic-inspired Grace Cathedral overlooks the city.

MAP 1 UNION SQUARE

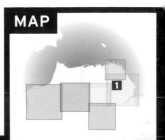

MAP

1

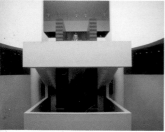

CHINATOWN/ FINANCIAL DISTRICT/ SOMA

Chinatown is the largest Chinese community out-side China. This fact is surprising in itself, but it's even more remarkable when you consider the series of discriminatory laws passed at the end of the 19th century. By 1853, an influx of immigrants flee-ing famine and war in their homeland gave rise to a phenomenally crowded, 12-block neighborhood clus-tered around Portsmouth Square. Today, the still-crowded streets and alleys are lined with dim sum palaces, cheap souvenir shops, and ornate temples. The neighboring Financial District is not as much of a tourist attraction, but visitors will be energized by a stroll through roughly 38 million square feet of prime office space.

Decades of urban renewal have transformed SoMa (South of Market) from a deteriorating industrial dis-trict into one of the most vibrant spots in town. Now in its full glory, SoMa boasts a thriving arts scene anchored by San Francisco Museum of Modern Art (SFMOMA) and Yerba Buena Center for the Arts. Just southeast of SoMa is the South Beach neighborhood dominated by the San Francisco Giants' retro-styled SBC Park.

MAP 2 CHINATOWN/FINANCIAL DISTRICT/SOMA   3.4

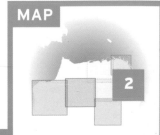

MAP

2

NORTH BEACH/
THE WATERFRONT

The oldest Italian enclave in the city, North Beach is still a thriving neighborhood, though these days visitors are as likely to see tai chi practitioners as bocce ball aficionados in Washington Square. Still, the district offers an impressive array of both family-style and more upscale Italian restaurants, and the area's cafés are legendary centers of poetry, conversation, and damned good coffee (there's not a Starbucks in sight). Stroll Columbus Avenue for a hint of the neighborhood's irresistible charms or ascend Telegraph Hill to the historic Coit Tower for breathtaking 360-degree views of San Francisco and the bay. At the opposite end of the zone, drive down the landscaped, hairpin curves of Lombard Street.

Tracing the long curve where city meets bay, the waterfront is a varied swath of the city. Fisherman's Wharf, once a bustling port is now a slightly kitschy approximation of what it used to be. Pier 39 is a circus like imitation of a waterfront marketplace, but does offer some great street performers and nearby sightseeing tours of the bay and Alcatraz Island. For a break from the wharf crowds, walk southeast along the Embarcadero, recently reborn as a palm-lined haven for walkers, bicyclists, runners, and skaters.

MAP 3 NORTH BEACH/THE WATERFRONT

19

17

15

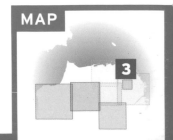

MAP

3

MARINA/COW HOLLOW/ PACIFIC HEIGHTS

Much of what is now the Marina district didn't exist until after the devastating earthquake and fires of 1906. Elegant townhouses were built atop the landfill, and the Marina became one of the city's most desirable neighborhoods. The Marina was hit again by the Loma Prieta earthquake of 1989, but the neighborhood rebounded quickly, becoming once again a yuppie stronghold dense with upscale shops and restaurants. The refurbished Palace of Fine Arts also continues to stand strong – a symbol of the neighborhood's prevailing character.

Just inland from the Marina district is Cow Hollow, named for the dairy farms established here in the mid-1800s. After the Gold Rush, this area became a fashionable place to live. The cows were ordered out, and San Francisco's elite moved in, building impressive Victorian homes. Neatly dividing the affluent neighborhood, Union Street, once home to hardware stores and barbershops, is now a stylish shopping promenade.

Perched high above Cow Hollow, Pacific Heights is one of the city's most exclusive residential neighborhoods. The stately mansions here are home to wealthy families, many of whom frequent the upper Fillmore Street, where tony boutiques and gourmet bistros draw serious shoppers and diners.

MAP 4 MARINA/COW HOLLOW/PACIFIC HEIGHTS

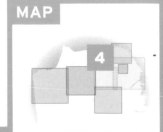

MAP

4

CIVIC CENTER/ HAYES VALLEY

The Civic Center's political and cultural import is undeniable – here you'll find the sumptuous City Hall, the stately War Memorial Opera House, and the modernist Davies Symphony Hall, to name just a few of the buildings between Franklin, Hyde, Hayes, and McAllister Streets. But if a city is a body and its center is the heart, then this heart suffers from a kind of coronary bypass – life seems to have been diverted elsewhere. Things liven up when the United Nations Plaza fills with protesters or farmers – don't miss the farmers market, which bursts into being on Wednesdays and Sundays.

Centered on Hayes Street between Franklin and Laguna, Hayes Valley is where opera-goers grab a bite to eat after the show. The swells still come, but so now does everyone else. Hayes Valley has gone upscale so fast that locals' heads are still spinning. Thankfully, the new establishments are all small, quirky, and independent. They include galleries, high-end home decor shops, funky shoe stores, and boutiques that'll make you wish you had more discretionary income. Just up the hill is lovely Alamo Square, a pretty park bordered by postcard-perfect Victorians.

MAP 5 CIVIC CENTER/HAYES VALLEY

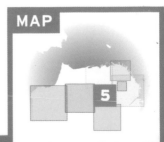

MAP

5

MISSION/CASTRO/ NOE VALLEY

With its mix of Latino immigrants, working artists, and SUV-driving professionals, the Mission is a neighborhood bursting at the seams with idiosyncratic energy. Changing block to block, the zone manages to be blue collar, edgy, and gentrified all at once. The heart of the neighborhood is still very much Latin American, with delicious burritos and *pupusas* around every corner. Visit the historic Mission Dolores for a lesson on the city's earliest beginnings.

Several blocks west, the Castro district blasted out of the closet in the 1970s to become the grand dame of San Francisco neighborhoods. Once a conservative, working-class area, this mecca for gay men is now known for its racy and rambunctious parades, festivals, and after-hours entertainment. It's also a great place to eat, shop, and people-watch.

Next door is Noe Valley, a relaxed but bustling neighborhood whose sidewalks are crowded with pets and strollers. Irish and German immigrants flocked here in the 1880s, lured by richly embellished Victorians that could be had for as little as $800. The immigrants' legacy survives in a few local pubs, but the neighborhood has gone upscale with high-end vintage boutiques and designer furniture stores.

MAP 6 MISSION/CASTRO/NOE VALLEY

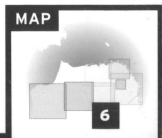

MAP

6

THE HAIGHT/ INNER SUNSET/ INNER RICHMOND

Haight-Ashbury (locally known as "the Haight") is best known for the wave of counterculture energy that broke here in the 1960s. The area became a magnet for drifters, dropouts, and visionaries who preached (and practiced) a heady blend of peace, love, and psychedelic drugs. If the door to the promised new consciousness never swung fully open, it nevertheless remains ajar here today, where head shops and tie-dye emporiums hold their own even as chain stores like the Gap move in.

Bordering the south and north sides of Golden Gate Park, the Sunset and the Richmond sit squarely in the fog belt. Once nothing but sand, these neighborhoods were born in the 1920s when developers paved over the dunes and built cookie-cutter single-family homes that sold for around $5,000 apiece. While the Outer Sunset is still primarily residential, the Inner Sunset, especially around Irving Street and 9th Avenue, is dense with restaurants and cafés, independent art galleries, and quirky boutiques. The Richmond, like the Sunset, is divided into Inner and Outer; the Inner is the livelier zone, especially on Clement Street, between Arguello and 12th Avenue.

MAP 7 THE HAIGHT/INNER SUNSET/INNER RICHMOND

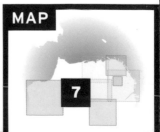

MAP

7

GOLDEN GATE PARK

A tranquil oasis in the midst of a metropolis, Golden Gate Park offers up more than a thousand acres of sparkling lakes, exotic gardens, and a dizzying array of recreational opportunities. Stretching more than three miles from the Haight to the Pacific, this is one of the largest man-made parks in the world, and is certainly among the most inviting. The park is designed to provide visitors with a gradual transition from city to ocean, so many of the main attractions are located on the eastern end, near the Haight, Inner Sunset, and Inner Richmond neighborhoods. Once the centerpiece of the 1894 Midwinter International Exposition, the Music Concourse area remains the cultural heart of Golden Gate Park.

Bordering the western end of the park, the Outer Sunset and Outer Richmond, both primarily residential neighborhoods, hold a sense of remoteness that increases the closer you get to the Pacific Ocean, the city's westernmost boundary. Once you reach Ocean Beach, a drive north along the coast leads you to the Palace of the Legion of Honor, a neoclassical-style museum that houses a collection spanning more than 4,000 years of fine art history. Stop in the nearby Cliff House for dinner and a sunset view of the spectacular coastline.

MAP 8 GOLDEN GATE PARK

15TH

P 7

AVE

Lake

16TH

AVE

AVE

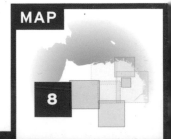

MAP

8

★ SIGHTS

SFMOMA
★38

★32
YERBA BUENA
GARDENS

MAP 1 | UNION SQUARE

CABLE CARS

San Francisco's famed cable cars are slow, antiquated, and impractical as a means of transportation. These very qualities make riding them one of the best ways to experience this fast-paced, high-tech, auto-clogged city. You get to relish the journey, while time and destination become almost inconsequential.

Prior to cable cars, San Francisco's steep grades could be scaled only by horse-drawn streetcars. Heavy loads on rain-slicked cobblestones caused frequent, grisly accidents. After witnessing one such catastrophe, Andrew Smith Hallidie vowed to find a better way to climb the city's hills. Using his father's invention, the wire rope, Hallidie connected a pulley system to a streetcar. On August 2, 1873, his first cable car cruised down Nob Hill. Within a month, the Clay Street Line began public service, igniting a citywide cable-car craze.

Modernization soon forced cable cars the way of horse-drawn carriages. After the 1906 earthquake, most lines went electric. And by the 1940s, cable cars were nearly extinct. Citizens rallied to save the remaining lines, and in 1964, the federal government declared the cars National Historic Landmarks.

Today, cable cars traverse some of San Francisco's most scenic neighborhoods. Two of the three lines begin at the Powell/Market turnaround near Union Square. The Powell-Mason route runs up and over Nob Hill to Bay Street at Fisherman's Wharf, while the Powell-Hyde line climbs Nob and Russian Hills before ending at Aquatic Park. The California Street route begins in the Financial District, running through Chinatown and over Nob Hill to Van Ness Avenue. Tickets cost $3 and are purchased at turnaround points or onboard.

 F4✪60 CABLE CAR TOURNAROUND, POWELL ST. AT MARKET
415-673-6864
HOURS: DAILY 6:30 A.M.-12:30 A.M.

GRACE CATHEDRAL

Perched atop posh Nob Hill, this grand architectural marvel humbly claims service as a house of prayer for all. Despite the rhetoric, Grace Cathedral is no Glide Memorial, which provides ministry, hot meals, and medical services to the city's most down-and-out. Indeed, Grace Cathedral

CABLE CARS

GRACE CATHEDRAL

is a playground for city socialites. As the saying goes, Grace Cathedral is where God stays when He visits San Francisco.

Grace Cathedral descends from Grace Church, which opened in 1849 as a clapboard chapel on Powell Street. By 1862, a brick church had replaced the chapel and the congregation included some of San Francisco's most prominent families. The 1906 fires destroyed the building, but two mansions at the peak of Nob Hill also burned and the property was donated to the Episcopal Diocese. In 1910, Lewis P. Hobart was named cathedral architect and a $2.7 million fund drive fueled construction until 1933, when the Great Depression halted work. Grace Cathedral finally reopened in 1964.

From the outside, the cathedral's ornate towers cast an exalted, somewhat intimidating, presence. Its great stairs lead to the 16-foot Doors of Paradise, which are exact replicas of the original entry to the baptistry of the cathedral in Florence, Italy. Inside, a vaulted ceiling and towering pillars soar 91 feet above wooden pews, and a kaleidoscope of colors stream through stained-glass windows.

Yet, this is no ordinary church. The stained-glass windows feature images of John Glenn, Albert Einstein, and Robert Frost. Guest speakers have included Dr. Martin Luther King, Jr., Jane Goodall, and the Dalai Lama. Indoor and outdoor labyrinths invite quiet reflection, and the AIDS Interfaith Chapel showcases an altarpiece by artist Keith Haring.

  1100 CALIFORNIA ST. 415-749-6300
HOURS: MON.-FRI. 7 A.M.-5:45 P.M., SAT. AND SUN. 8 A.M.-5 P.M.

MAP 2 CHINATOWN/FINANCIAL DISTRICT/SOMA

CHINATOWN

San Francisco's Chinatown is an explosion of sights, sounds, and scents. Colorful produce stands, spirited bargaining matches, incense-infused temples, and kitschy souvenir shops fill its narrow streets. While Chinatown is only steps from the posh shops of Union Square, the designer suits of the Financial District, and the garlic-laden pastas of North Beach, a visit here is a journey across the Pacific.

Early Chinese immigrants arrived in San Francisco in the mid-1800s. Many of them opened laundries, restaurants, pharmacies, and markets to meet the needs of the Gold Rush boomtown. Some 12 blocks of tenements, temples, and shops housed more than 22,000 immigrants united by heritage, language, and financial interdependence. In the 1860s, Chinese laborers were recruited to build the transcontinental railroad. In 1869, when the railway neared completion, thousands were suddenly jobless and targeted by some of the most discriminatory laws in American history. In response, Chinatown grew defiantly stronger as a homogenous, self-sustaining community. When the 1906 fires burned the neighborhood to the ground, Western architects rebuilt it with an emphasized Asian flair, complete with dragon lampposts and pagoda roofs, to attract tourists.

To explore Chinatown, begin at the intersection of Bush Street and Grant Avenue, where a dragon-crested archway leads into a sea of plastic Buddhas and other tourist treasures. For a more authentic shopping experience, visit Stockton Street, where markets feature victuals that still hop, quack, swim, and flop. Watch fortunes being made at the Golden Gate Fortune Cookie Factory on Ross Alley, or spend a moment of reflection in a temple on Waverly Place.

MAP 2 A2**2** START AT DRAGON GATES, GRANT AVE. AT BUSH ST.

SBC PARK

Everyone loves a ballpark. That must have been the mantra when Giants owners, riding a national wave of new vintage-style parks, commissioned their new home in 1997. Mixing nostalgia for America's favorite pastime with

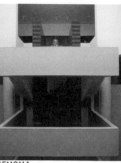

CHINATOWN   SBC PARK   SFMOMA

state-of-the-art amenities, SBC Park pulls in the crowds while living up to the hype.

The nation's first privately financed major league ballpark in more than 35 years, SBC Park opened to adoring fans in 2000. The debut meant a new home for the Giants, but also symbolized the rebirth of San Francisco's long-neglected waterfront. The ballpark was built so close to the water that homeruns regularly splash into the bay at McCovey Cove. Inside, the smell of garlic permeates the air, a reminder that Giants fans – with cell phones and Palm Pilots in hand – enjoy the finer things in life. While hot dogs and peanuts are readily available, minibistros and upscale chain restaurants dish up sushi, fruit smoothies, espressos, microbrews, and California wines.

As the name "Giants" suggests, everything here is larger than life. Twenty-four palm trees line the park entrance, a tribute to the jersey number of Giants legend, Willie Mays. A massive baseball glove looms beyond left field. A more controversial highlight is an 80-foot Coca-Cola bottle, home to tubular slides designed for kids of all ages.

While tickets are often scarce, seats can be found. Every game day, 500 bleacher seats are released for sale, along with a few prime unclaimed seats. During the off-season, ballpark tours are available.

 MAP 2 D5●63   24 WILLIE MAYS PLAZA 415-972-2000 (TICKET RESERVATIONS), 415-972-2400 (TOUR INFORMATION) HOURS: DAILY 10 A.M.–2 P.M. (EVENTS PERMITTING)

SFMOMA/YERBA BUENA GARDENS

Distinguished by its circular, black-and-white stone tower, SFMOMA (San Francisco Museum of Modern Art) is widely considered the West Coast's most comprehensive resource for modern and contemporary art. Designed by renowned Swiss architect Mario Botta, this striking,

Before heading over to SFMOMA, stop in **Yank Sing (p. 28)** for some of the best dim sum in town. After browsing the museum's most recent collections and enjoying a respite in the neighboring Yerba Buena Gardens, walk over to the nearby entertainment center **Metreon (p. 81).** Cruise the various high-tech gadget stores there or catch a movie on one of the 16 movie screens. For a romantic dinner, walk a few blocks down Howard Street to a small brick alley (Hawthorne St.) where you'll find **Hawthorne Lane (p. 26)**; sit at the low-lit bar and order from the well-priced café menu. Finish off the evening with drinks at neighboring lounge/gallery **111 Minna (p. 46)**, where you can browse art while sipping on your after-dinner Manhattan.

modernist building houses works by well-known artists like Henri Matisse, Diego Rivera, Jackson Pollock, Richard Diebenkorn, and Ansel Adams, along with a spectacular lineup of special exhibits.

Just across the street, the Yerba Buena Gardens consists of more than 85 acres of cascading gardens, world-renowned museums, trendy restaurants, high-tech amusements, and hip lofts. At the heart of the development is The Esplanade, a 5.5-acre park featuring a 22-foot-high waterfall memorial to civil rights leader Dr. Martin Luther King, Jr. The Esplanade is also home to the Yerba Buena Center for the Arts, which presents dance performances, international film festivals, and open-air concerts. Opening in the summer of 2005 is the $11 million Museum of the African Diaspora.

Above the Esplanade, gracing the top of Moscone Center, The Rooftop at Yerba Buena Gardens transforms an entire city block into a children's wonderland. Highlights include an NHL-regulation-size ice rink, a 1906 carousel, and a bowling alley. Zeum, a multimedia production studio, offers kids the opportunity to direct and star in their own creations.

MAP 2 C4✪38 SFMOMA: 151 3RD ST. 415-357-4000
HOURS: FRI.-TUES. 11 A.M.-5:45 P.M., THURS. 11 A.M.-8:45 P.M. (CLOSED ON WED.)

MAP 2 C3✪32 YERBA BUENA GARDENS: 3RD ST. BTWN. MISSION AND FOLSOM STS. 415-543-1718 (ARTS AND EVENTS INFORMATION)

FERRY BUILDING
Anchoring the foot of Market Street, the 1896 Ferry Building's 240-foot Victorian clock tower is modeled after Spain's Giralda Cathedral Tower. Reopened in 2003 after a multi-million-dollar renovation, the building continues to serve as the main ferry hub.

MAP 2 A5✪12 1 FERRY BLDG.
415-291-3276

TRANSAMERICA PYRAMID   ALCATRAZ ISLAND

OLD MINT

This 1874 Greek-revival landmark is on the National Trust for Historic Preservation's "Most Endangered List." The site of a proposed museum of San Francisco, the "Granite Lady" sits derelict, but still glorious.

 MAP 2 D2 ✪46   5TH AND MISSION STS.

TRANSAMERICA PYRAMID

At 853 feet, the tallest building in the city rises 48 floors, spans almost an entire city block, and even boasts a pleasant mini-park shaded by redwoods.

 MAP 2 A3 ✪7   600 MONTGOMERY ST.

MAP 3 | NORTH BEACH/THE WATERFRONT

ALCATRAZ ISLAND

Once uninhabitable save for its namesake *alcatraces* (Spanish for seabirds), Alcatraz Island has since been home to a number of inhabitants, including Union defenders, military deserters, real-life gangsters, and American Indian activists. Now part of the Golden Gate National Recreation Area, "the Rock" welcomes more than 1.3 million visitors a year.

Best known for its "escape-proof" federal prison, Alcatraz underwent its first transformation during the 1849 Gold Rush and became a citadel protecting San Francisco's newfound riches from pirating vessels. Fortress Alcatraz later defended California from the Confederates during the Civil War and served time as a military prison until 1933.

When the military prison closed, FBI director J. Edgar Hoover targeted Alcatraz as the inescapable prison that would house notorious Mafia leaders. Soon, gangsters like Al Capone, George "Machine Gun" Kelly, and Robert "The Birdman of Alcatraz" Stroud arrived. Sheer cliffs, treacherous tides, and frigid water kept escape attempts to a minimum — and no attempt is believed to have succeeded.

The maximum-security prison closed in 1963, and Alcatraz Island remained largely deserted until a group of American Indians took control in 1969. They occupied Alcatraz for more than a year, demanding the deed to the island. Though ultimately unsuccessful, their bold efforts helped ignite the larger Native American movement.

Today, Alcatraz is but a short ferry ride from Pier 41. While many come seeking fun in the sun, the experience can be reflective, somber, and even a little chilling. Highlights include audio cell-house tours, interpretive walks, and informative video presentations.

 B3⊕4 PIER 41 415-705-5555 (TICKET RESERVATIONS)
HOURS: FERRIES EVERY HALF HOUR BEGINNING 9:30 AND
10:15 A.M. UNTIL 4:15 P.M. (SUMMER) AND UNTIL 2:15 P.M.
(WINTER)

COIT TOWER

The legacy of a legendary San Francisco personality, Coit Tower rises a bold 210 feet atop Telegraph Hill. The perfect starting point for a tour of San Francisco, this city icon is visible from most spots in San Francisco and across the bay. The story behind Coit Tower begins with eccentric heiress Elizabeth Wyche "Lillie" Hitchcock.

Growing up on Telegraph Hill in the mid-1800s, Lillie developed an everlasting passion for fire stations, fire engines, and firefighters — even receiving honorary membership in the Knickerbocker Engine Company No. 5 fire department. While she often raised eyebrows among the social set by playing poker, shooting guns, and smoking cigars, Lillie's quick wit and unique flair made her the adored life of the party until her death in 1929. In her will, Lillie left San Francisco $118,000 for "adding to the beauty of the city I have always loved." And on October 8, 1933, Coit Tower — resembling the nozzle of a fire hose — opened to the public amid great fanfare.

Inside the main entrance, frescoes vibrantly depict life during the Great Depression. The murals, a product of the New Deal's Works Progress Administration, are widely acclaimed for their reflection of Diego Rivera's social realist style. For a 360-degree viewpoint, visitors can take an elevator to the top of the tower, where a circular room overlooks the city.

COIT TOWER   FISHERMAN'S WHARF

Surrounded by cottages nestled against the slopes
of Telegraph Hill, Coit Tower is accessible via precari-
ously rising stone and wooden footpaths. Other options
include driving (though parking is limited) and public
transportation.

 MAP 3 **D4 ○15** 1 TELEGRAPH HILL BLVD. 415-362-0808
HOURS: DAILY 10 A.M.-5 P.M.
TOURS: SAT. 11 A.M.

FISHERMAN'S WHARF

Equal parts old-fashioned boardwalk, historic fishing village, and commercialized amusement park, Fisherman's
Wharf offers a circus of quick-witted street performers, "I
Love San Francisco" T-shirts, catch-of-the-day dining, and
mindless entertainment. Designed with the traveling plea-
sure-seeker in mind, this is the place locals love to hate.
Yet even tried-and-true cynics forced to entertain out-of-
town guests can't help but enjoy themselves here.

Much of the action centers at Pier 39. More than 110
shops, selling everything from kitschy souvenirs to original artwork, line the two-level plaza. Acclaimed restaurants offer sweeping bay views, and a colorful bevy of
jugglers, magicians, and musicians attract the wide-eyed
attention of camera-toting families. Pier 39 is also the
departure point for Angel Island and other narrated bay
jaunts. And just a few feet from the water's edge, hundreds of sea lions unabashedly bark, swim, and sunbathe,
much to the delight of enraptured audiences.

Moving west along the waterfront, visitors catch the
aroma of boiling Dungeness crab and fresh fish wafting
from restaurants, cafés, and grottos. San Francisco got
its start as a seaport, and today hundreds of independent and commercial fishing boats call Fisherman's Wharf
home. While a wide variety of fish are caught off the
San Francisco coast, crab remains an enduring favorite.

9

LOMBARD STREET   PALACE OF FINE ARTS

During the height of crab season (mid-November through June), much of the catch is purchased immediately by local restaurants and food vendors, who cook the meat in steaming cauldrons or serve it in recipes that date back to San Francisco's earliest settlers.

 MAP 3 B2❷2 BTWN. PIER 39 AND AQUATIC PARK

LOMBARD STREET

You've no doubt seen it in movies, on TV, and on post-cards – Lombard Street, otherwise known as "the crookedest street in the world." So, why bother braving the bumper-to-bumper cars navigating its zigzag turns? For one, you can't beat the view from the top. With its 27-percent grade, Lombard Street offers unobstructed vistas of the San Francisco Bay, Alcatraz Island, Fisherman's Wharf, Coit Tower, and the city. For another, this red-brick road, situated between tony mansions and luxurious town homes, offers a glimpse into San Francisco's trademark extravagance and eccentricity.

Tucked between Hyde and Leavenworth Streets, this whimsical block was built for a very practical purpose: to help residents navigate the almost impossibly steep Russian Hill. In 1922, city planners carved eight switch-backs into the hill. They made one stipulation: Property owners were responsible for the greenery between the curves. With residents unable to agree on a landscaping plan, Lombard Street soon became overgrown with juniper and other shrubs, much to the chagrin of neighbor Peter Bercut, a French millionaire and former city parks commissioner. In 1947, Bercut and his butler uprooted the jungle; he then had 2,000 hydrangea plants shipped from France. The hydrangeas continue to bloom along this quaint lane in brilliant hues of pink, blue, and white.

For convenience during the peak summer months, take a cable car directly to the top of Lombard Street and walk down the noncurvy stairs on either side. The bottom of the hill offers one of Lombard Street's most picture-perfect vantage points.

 D1 ✪9   LOMBARD ST. BTWN. HYDE AND LEAVENWORTH STS. (CARS ENTER ON HYDE ST. SIDE)

FILBERT STREET INCLINE

Boasting a 31.5 percent gradient, this part of Filbert is the steepest street in a city known for its hills. Test your driving skills and cruise down the street for a quick thrill.

 E1 ✪19   FILBERT ST. BTWN. LEAVENWORTH AND HYDE STS.

MAP 4 | MARINA/COW HOLLOW/PACIFIC HEIGHTS

PALACE OF FINE ARTS

In a city that has withstood some truly devastating losses – from the ravaging fires of 1906 to the AIDS epidemic of the 1980s and 1990s and the Loma Prieta earthquake of 1989 – the Palace of Fine Arts is yet another survivor. Built as a temporary structure for the 1915 Panama-Pacific International Exhibit, it has been rebuilt, refurbished, and retrofitted, and today stands as a reminder of the city's enduring spirit.

Renowned architect Bernard R. Maybeck designed the Palace of Fine Arts as a romanticized interpretation of a Roman ruin, conjuring the beauty and contemplative melancholy of the fine art it would display. As one of the fair's 11 temporary exhibit palaces, it was inexpensively built using stucco, wood, and chicken wire. In 1965, however, 95 percent of the deteriorating structure was demolished, then rebuilt using more permanent materials. Today, its theater hosts a variety of cultural and educational events, including film festivals, concerts, lectures, and performing arts.

Although the Palace of Fine Arts no longer displays the works of art that Maybeck originally envisioned, it does celebrate another form of human achievement – scientific discovery. The Exploratorium, a hands-on science museum with more than 650 interactive displays, invites you to feel your way through a series of shapes and textures in the pitch-black tactile dome, take a picture of your shadow, touch a tornado, talk into an echo tube, and

STAIRWAY STREETS

There are more than 300 stairway streets hidden around San Francisco, providing both a practical means for navigating some of the steepest inclines and a chance to peek into a hidden side of the city. Many are concentrated in North Beach, around Telegraph Hill, including the the Vallejo Street Stairway (btwn. Montgomery and Sansome Sts.). Two of most delightful are the **Lyon Street Steps (p. 12)** and the **Filbert Street Incline (p. 11)**, a charming three-block stairway that winds through a secret wonderland of cottages and gardens. The Castro district also shelters several excellent stairway streets, including the Vulcan Steps (btwn. Ord and Levant Sts.) and the Saturn Street Stairs (connecting Ord and Saturn Sts.).

grow and shrink in a distorted room. The museum also hosts educational series, art exhibits, exploratory film festivals, and other special events.

 C1❍20 3301 LYON ST. 415-567-6642
HOURS: DAILY 10 A.M.-6 P.M., WED. 10 A.M.-9 P.M.
(MEMORIAL DAY-LABOR DAY); TUES.-SUN. 10 A.M.-5 P.M.
(LABOR DAY-MEMORIAL DAY)

FORT MASON
This vibrant waterfront arts complex was an important military base for more than 200 years. Now part of the Golden Gate National Recreation Area, Fort Mason provides the perfect mix of culture and nature.

 B4❍12 MARINA BLVD. AT BUCHANAN ST.
415-345-7544 (RECORDED VISITOR INFORMATION LINE)

HAAS-LILIENTHAL HOUSE
The only intact private home with its original furnishings from San Francisco's Victorian era, this 1896 house-museum affords visitors a glimpse into a bygone age.

MAP 4 E5❍55 2007 FRANKLIN ST.
415-441-3000

LYON STREET STEPS
While the ultimate goal of ascending these 291 steps is the stunning view of the Palace of Fine Arts and the bay, the path's manicured gardens remind visitors to stop and smell the flowers.

MAP 4 E1❍49 LYON ST. BTWN. GREEN ST. AND BROADWAY

OCTAGON HOUSE
Built during a temporary craze for eight-sided houses, this 1861 structure is open for tours three times a month (noon-3 P.M. on the second and fourth Thursday and second Sunday of the

FORT MASON   ALAMO SQUARE/PAINTED LADIES

month). The city's other surviving octagon (at 1067 Green St.) is closed to the public.

 D5 ✪41   2645 GOUGH ST.
415-441-7512

THE PRESIDIO

Once home to Ohlone Native Americans, the Presidio now features nearly 500 historic buildings that narrate the story of more than 200 years of military history. Inside the wooded park, 11 miles of hiking trails and 14 miles of paved roads weave through native plant habitats, coastal bluffs, concrete bunkers, sandy beaches, and gracious homes.

 C1 ✪22   LOMBARD ST. AT LYON ST. (LOMBARD GATE ENTRANCE)
415-561-5300

MAP 5 CIVIC CENTER/HAYES VALLEY

ALAMO SQUARE/PAINTED LADIES

As decadent as any Castro Street parade, as upscale as any Union Square boutique, the "Painted Ladies," bedecked in vibrant colors and gingerbread trim, are quintessential San Francisco. And unlike hippie ponchos or power ties, these ladies never go out of style.

Victorian architecture made its San Francisco debut in the early 1850s, and by 1900 a reported 48,000 Victorian homes, designed in the romanticized Italianate, Stick, Queen Anne, and Edwardian styles, graced the city's streets. Sadly, fires from the 1906 earthquake destroyed thousands of them. The flames stopped at Van Ness Avenue, sparing neighborhoods to the west, including Eureka Valley (now the Castro), Noe Valley, Haight-Ashbury, Pacific Heights, and Cow Hollow. While many Victorians suffered from neglect during the 1950s flight

CITY HALL

MISSION DOLORES

to the suburbs, they quickly regained their coveted status, undergoing meticulous restoration.

One of the best places to experience the city's vibrant Victorians is along the cypress-shaded paths of Alamo Square. Directly across from the park, along the 700 block of Steiner Street, a gently ascending row of perfectly detailed Victorians provides a magnificent contrast to the backdrop of San Francisco's cityscape. Known as the Six Sisters, these gabled Queen Anne starlets have appeared in movies, television shows, and commercials, and frequently grace postcards and travel guide covers – earning them the nickname "Postcard Row."

Visitors needn't admire the Painted Ladies from a distance. Alamo Square is surrounded by several charming Victorian bed-and-breakfasts offering accommodations that range from cozy to opulent.

 MAP 5 D2 ✪ 21   STEINER ST. BTWN. FULTON AND HAYES STS.

CITY HALL

The crown jewel of San Francisco, an exquisitely restored beaux-arts masterpiece stands taller than the U.S. Capitol, its glittering gold dome visible from many parts of the city. Regardless of its lofty stature, the building remains as colorful and tumultuous as the city it serves, having hosted everything from political riots to Marilyn Monroe's wedding to Joe DiMaggio.

Mayor James "Sunny" Rolph inaugurated the current city hall in 1915, after the previous location was destroyed in the 1906 earthquake. Meticulously hand-drawn by renowned architect Arthur Brown, Jr., it cost nearly $3.5 million to build and encompassed two city blocks. In its years of service, City Hall was the backdrop for numerous political controversies – including the 1978 assassinations of Mayor George Moscone and gay Supervisor Harvey

Milk — until its devastation in 1989 by the Loma Prieta earthquake.

City Hall reopened a decade later, after a four-year, $300 million seismic retrofit, high-tech modernization, and historic restoration project initiated by then-mayor Willie Brown. His successor, Mayor Gavin Newsom took office in January 2004, and a month later brought City Hall and San Francisco back into the national spotlight by allowing the city to issue marriage licenses to same-sex couples. Thousands of same-sex couples rushed to City Hall to legalize their unions and participate in the big celebration. Although the California Supreme Court eventually ruled that the city did not have the authority to issue the nearly 4,000 licenses, City Hall remains a site of pride for many.

Visitors shouldn't miss the chance to see the grand marble staircase and light-filled rotunda, or take a ride in the restored birdcage elevators and peek into the offices of the mayor and the city supervisors.

MAP 5 D5✪47 1 DR. CARLTON B. GOODLETT PL.
415-554-6023 (DOCENT TOURS)
HOURS: MON.–FRI. 8 A.M.–8 P.M., SAT. NOON–4 P.M.

CATHEDRAL OF ST. MARY OF THE ASSUMPTION
This 1971 strikingly modern white cathedral dominates the surrounding skyline and serves as San Francisco's Archdiocese of the Catholic Church. From inside, soaring windows provide a stunning view of the city.

MAP 5 B4✪12 1111 GOUGH ST.
415-567-2020

PEACE PAGODA
Erected in 1968 as a symbol of friendship between Japan and the United States, this five-tiered structure and its surrounding plaza are the heart of one of the country's largest Japantowns.

MAP 5 B3✪11 POST ST. AT BUCHANAN ST.

MAP 6 | MISSION/CASTRO/NOE VALLEY

MISSION DOLORES
Steeped in historical and religious significance, Mision San Francisco de Asís, more commonly known as Mission Dolores, traces San Francisco's heritage to its beginnings. The 6th of 21 California missions established under the direction of Father Junipero Serra, beautifully preserved Mission Dolores is a reminder of the city's more pious origins.

Combine your tour of the Mission Dolores with an exploration of the surrounding energetic Mission district. **Dolores Park (p. 88),** one block from the church, provides beautiful views of downtown and is a great place to people-watch and soak up the sun. Stroll down to **Valencia Street (p. 69)** to browse the unique bookstores and boutiques, and stop into the nearby **Taquería Cancún (p. 38)** for a taste of the Mission's favorite burrito. Walk off your lunch on your way to **El Rio (p. 51)** or take the 14 bus line and get off at Cesár Chavez Blvd. Sip one of El Rio's famously strong margaritas on the patio (live salsa bands on Sundays from 4 P.M.-8 P.M.)

In 1769, Father Serra arrived in Alta California, then a Spanish province, on a mission to "civilize" Native Americans by converting them to Roman Catholicism. By 1791, the building of Mision San Francisco de Asís was complete. The complex eventually included a chapel, convent, granary, shops, servant quarters, graveyard, military housing, and central courtyard.

While many of the original buildings are gone, the chapel and cemetery remain open to the public. Surrounded by the highly urbanized Mission district, this historic landmark is a tranquil oasis of solemn, if somewhat haunting, beauty.

The chapel, though simple in design, is adorned with precious sculptures, decorative altars, and oil paintings. In the courtyard, a diorama created for the 1939 World's Fair depicts the mission as it appeared in 1791. While the adjacent basilica is breathtaking, the real highlight may be the cemetery. Weather-aged gravestones bear names that include Don Luis Antonio Arguello, the first governor of Alta California, and Don Francisco de Haro, the first mayor of San Francisco. Guided walking and audio tours are available for a small donation.

 B3✪12 3321 16TH ST. 415-621-8203
HOURS: DAILY 9 A.M.-4:30 P.M. (MAY-OCT.); DAILY 9 A.M.-4 P.M. (NOV.-APR.)

BALMY ALLEY
Begun in the 1970s as part of a city-sponsored public works project, this one-block-long alley is an explosion of colorful murals depicting Latin American political struggles and celebrating community action.

 E6✪65 BALMY ST. BTWN. 24TH AND 25TH STS.

WOMEN'S BUILDING
Covered in a glorious mural entitled *Maestrapeace*, the facade of this colorful building is the main highlight. Functioning as a multi-cultural center for women and girls, the building hosts many political meetings and benefit concerts.

 C4✪35 3543 18TH ST.
415-431-1180

CONSERVATORY
OF FLOWERS

GOLDEN GATE PARK

MAP 7 | THE HAIGHT/INNER SUNSET/INNER RICHMOND

CONSERVATORY OF FLOWERS

Reopened in 2003 after an eight-year renovation, the treasured Victorian landmark houses hundreds of exotic plants and flowers. A highlight is the Aquatic Plants exhibit, where beautiful pools of water feature floating flowers and giant lily pads.

MAP 7 D3✪13   JFK DR. AND CONSERVATORY DR.
415-666-7001

TEMPLE EMANU-EL

Designed by architect Arthur Brown, Jr., this 1926 temple culminates in a striking dome modeled after the Aya Sophia in Turkey.

MAP 7 A3✪2   2 LAKE ST.
415-751-2535

UNIVERSITY OF SAN FRANCISCO

Stroll through USF's 55-acre campus or hear a classical performance at the 1924 St. Ignatius Church. One of San Francisco's most beautiful buildings, its twin spires are visible from all over the city.

MAP 7 C4✪10   ENTER ON GOLDEN GATE AVE. BTWN. KITTREDGE AND
ROSELYN TERRACE 415-422-5555

MAP 8 | GOLDEN GATE PARK

GOLDEN GATE PARK

Encompassing more than a thousand acres of meadows, lakes, forests, and exotic gardens, Golden Gate Park provides plenty of refreshing green space and amusements for the urban dwellers and visitors it serves. Extending from Haight-Ashbury for more than three miles to the Pacific Ocean, the park makes a great spot for a long

PALACE OF THE LEGION OF
HONOR

GOLDEN GATE BRIDGE

walk or bike ride; plenty of marked trails and paved pathways intertwine the park's highlights. On weekends especially, the entire place is a hub of recreational pursuits,
with softball teams and Frisbee tossers sharing grassy
stretches with picnicking families.

Incredibly, this lushly landscaped haven, set aside by the
city in 1870, was coaxed out of barren, wind-swept sand
dunes. While the park's founder, William Hammond Hall,
was the first to bring the dunes under control using innovative sand-reclamation techniques, it was his hand-picked
successor, John Mclaren, who devoted most of his life to
the landscaping and development of the park. Thanks to
his foresight, winding pathways discourage speeding traffic, rich foliage attracts birds and wildlife, and more than a
million trees shelter visitors from harsh winds.

Some of the park's most popular attractions – the
Japanese Tea Garden, the Music Concourse, and the Bison
Paddock – were part of the 1894 Midwinter International
Exposition, Golden Gate Park's official opening extrava-
ganza. A century later, the park became famous for its
"Summer of Love" spectacles, including the 1967 Human
Be-In, and a few decades later, Jerry Garcia's funeral.

MAP 8 D4●15   STANYAN AT FELL ST. (MAIN ENTRANCE), JFK DR.
(MCLAREN LODGE VISITOR CENTER) 415-831-2700

PALACE OF THE LEGION OF HONOR

Situated atop an oceanfront bluff, the Palace of the Legion
of Honor houses a spectacular collection, spanning more
than 4,000 years of fine art history, which is equaled only
by its backdrop of rugged, sea-swept coastline.

The Legion of Honor opened on November 11, 1924. A
gift to the city from sugar baron Adolph Spreckles and
his wife Alma, this fine arts museum commemorates the

California servicemen who died during World War I. Built in French neoclassical style, the Palace is an exact, three-quarter-scale replica of the Palais de la Legion d'Honneur in Paris, where Napoleon Bonaparte paid tribute to French soldiers.

An avid patron of the arts, Alma Spreckles personally shaped the museum's early collections. She selectively acquired some of Auguste Rodin's most significant sculptures and also procured costume and set designs from the opera and ballet, as well as dance-related sculptures and drawings. Because of her artistic vision, the Legion of Honor is now one of the country's foremost repositories of theatrical design.

A colonnaded courtyard marks the entrance to the museum, providing a picturesque backdrop for an original casting of Rodin's *The Thinker*. Inside, more than 20 galleries display select works from a collection of more than 100,000 pieces, ranging from antiquities and decorative arts to impressionist masterpieces and modern sculptures. A 4,500-pipe organ built by the Ernest M. Skinner Company was incorporated into the museum's original design, and free recitals are presented every Saturday and Sunday at 4 P.M. Outside, near the reflecting pool, is George Segal's solemn *Holocaust* memorial sculpture.

 A3◑2 100 34TH AVE. 415-863-3330
HOURS: TUES.-SUN. 9:30 A.M.-5 P.M.

SUTRO BATHS

Built by Adolph Sutro at the end of the 19th century, this once-magnificent indoor swimming complex comprises ruins that invite exploration. Historical information is available at the Cliff House Visitor Center.

 B1◑5 POINT LOBOS AVE. AT GREAT HWY.
415-561-4323 (PRESIDIO VISITOR CENTER)

OVERVIEW MAP

GOLDEN GATE BRIDGE

With its graceful lines and striking vermilion color, this icon of art deco design is one of the world's most recognizable constructions. Yet the Golden Gate Bridge is as much an engineering feat as a work of art. Its twin 746-foot towers, giant steel arms, and 80,000 miles of cable provide the strength and flexibility to endure fierce Pacific storms and major earthquakes.

In 1872, railroad baron Charles Crocker presented the first plans for a bridge spanning the Golden Gate, an implausible challenge. And in 1916, structural engineer and journalist James H. Wilkins revived the concept in editorials calling for a bridge to connect the Bay Area's urban center with Marin's redwood wilds. His ideas caught on and city engineer Michael O'Shaughnessy initiated project studies. In 1929, Joseph Strauss became chief project engineer, and a year later, despite various opposition, voters approved a $35 million bond for a 1.7-mile, two-tiered suspension bridge. Work began in 1933 and Strauss's team of engineers, builders, and divers were soon contending with some acutely dangerous conditions – swift ocean currents, thick fog, and high winds. Finally, on May 27, 1937, the Golden Gate Bridge – painted International Orange to complement the natural surroundings – opened to a crowd of pedestrians.

Today, pedestrians still hold priveleged status, enjoying unparalleled views for free. To the north lie the rocky, wooded Marin Headlands, while the south offers spectacular views of the city. And 220 feet below, the Pacific meets the bay in a wave-churning canyon. Vista points on the northeast and southeast entrance corners provide more temperate but equally breathtaking views. Cars pay a $5 southbound toll.

OVERVIEW MAP B2 HIGHWAY 101 NORTH AT 415-921-5858
PEDESTRIAN WALKWAY HOURS: DAILY 6 A.M.-6 P.M.

TWIN PEAKS

Drive or hike up to this windswept vantage point – the highest peak in the city – for unforgettable panoramic views of San Francisco and the East and North Bays.

OVERVIEW MAP E3 FOLLOW TWIN PEAKS BLVD. OFF PORTOLA DR.

R RESTAURANTS

Hottest restaurant of the moment: **TOWN HALL,** p. 28

Most romantic restaurant: **LA FOLIE,** p. 33

Best patio: **FOREIGN CINEMA,** p. 36

Closest thing to Chez Panisse this side of the bridge:
QUINCE, p. 34

Best takeout: **THE GROVE,** p. 33

Best view with your veggies: **GREENS,** p. 33

Best place to feel stuffed: **SUPPENKÜCHE,** p. 35

Best three-figure splurge: **GARY DANKO,** p. 33

Coziest pizza place: **PIZZETTA 211,** p. 42

Best desserts: **TARTINE BAKERY,** p. 39

Longest brunch lines but worth the wait: **ELLA'S,** p. 32

PRICE KEY

$ ENTRÉES UNDER $10

$$ ENTRÉES BETWEEN $10 AND $20

$$$ ENTRÉES OVER $20

MAP 1 UNION SQUARE

ANZU *BUSINESS • SUSHI/STEAK* $$$
The refined, tranquil Anzu takes the concept of yin and yang into
uncharted territory. Not only do the sushi creations rival those of
the best Japanese restaurants, they make a delightful complement
to the menu's other specialty, prime aged steaks from Allen Brothers
of Chicago.

MAP 1 E3 ℞ 56 222 MASON ST. (HOTEL NIKKO)
415-394-1100

B44 *BUSINESS • CATALAN* $$
At lunchtime, this Catalan bistro is crammed with suits, seated in the
chic dining room or outside on an alley lined with European cafés.
Come dinner, the noise subsides. Choose a rioja to go with one of
the eight paella options.

MAP 1 B6 ℞ 12 44 BELDEN PL.
415-986-6287

CAFÉ CLAUDE *CAFÉ • FRENCH* $
With a wait staff imported directly from France, this charming bistro
is a Parisian delight. Live jazz and an extensive wine list perfectly
complement the delicately succulent menu, which includes *soupe à
l'oignon gratinée, baguette avec brie,* and *quiche aux legumes.*

MAP 1 C5 ℞ 23 7 CLAUDE LN.
415-392-3515

CAMPTON PLACE *ROMANTIC • CALIFORNIA-MEDITERRANEAN* $$$
Presentation is key for 20-something chef Daniel Humm, who cre-
ates works of art with dishes like wild Mediterranean *branzino* (sea
bass) and zucchini-wrapped squab. The elegant dining room, com-
plete with deep plush booths, provides the perfect spot to appreci-
ate his masterpieces.

MAP 1 C4 ℞ 20 340 STOCKTON ST. (CAMPTON PLACE HOTEL)
415-955-5555

CORTEZ *HOT SPOT • MEDITERRANEAN* $$
San Francisco restaurateur extraordinaire Pascal Rigo has elevated
the casual hotel restaurant to new levels with his latest venture.
Date- and mint-crusted lamb, plump crab cakes, and shoestring fries
with zippy Moroccan dips pair with creative cocktails in this loft-like,
comfortable space.

MAP 1 D2 ℞ 36 550 GEARY ST. (HOTEL ADAGIO)
415-292-6360

DOTTIE'S TRUE BLUE CAFE *BREAKFAST AND BRUNCH • AMERICAN* $
This classic Tenderloin joint garners adoration and acclaim from
its devotees by doling out massive three-egg omelets, fat slices of
French toast, homemade breads, and cinnamon-swirled streusel coffeecake. Stuff yourself silly.

MAP 1 E1 ℞ 54 522 JONES ST.
415-885-2767

B44

GRAND CAFÉ

FARALLON *BUSINESS • SEAFOOD* $$$

This temple of coastal cuisine consists of the Jelly Bar, the Nautilus
Room, and the main dining room, which once housed a swimming
pool. Each is a splendid seascape, the perfect backdrop for Farallon's
daily menu – artful renderings of the ocean's bounty – and its indulgent raw bar.

MAP 1 D3 R 41   450 POST ST.
415-956-6969

FIRST CRUSH *ROMANTIC • CALIFORNIA* $$

In vintner's terms, the first crush is the most dramatic moment
of the harvest. At the bar, take advantage of a pre-theater, three-
course prix fixe and flight of wine. In the romantic, purple and mus-
tard-colored dining room, seasonal entrées pair with bottles from
the California-centric stock.

MAP 1 E3 R 58   101 CYRIL MAGNIN ST.
415-982-7874

FLEUR DE LYS *ROMANTIC • FRENCH* $$$

Famous for its mammoth garden-tent venue, Fleur de Lys has been
the site of wedding proposals and celebrations for more than 30
years. Esteemed chef Hubert Keller creates bold and beautiful
French fare in three-, four-, and five-course spreads. Tasting and
vegetarian menus are also available.

MAP 1 C1 R 14   777 SUTTER ST.
415-673-7779

GRAND CAFÉ *ROMANTIC • CALIFORNIA-FRENCH* $$$

The Hotel Monaco's majestic ballroom-cum-art gallery – complete
with early-20th-century–style murals, trompe l'oeil, and modern
sculpture – provides the backdrop for celebratory California-French
feasting. Start with the duck confit, and move on to roasted rack of
lamb or sautéed skate wing.

MAP 1 D2 R 38   501 GEARY ST.
415-292-0101

HANA ZEN *BUSINESS • JAPANESE* $$

This sleek and stylish restaurant offers one of the most engaging,
extensive Japanese menus in town, including one sparkling rarity,
authentic yakitori, or grilled fowl. À la carte standouts include a

POSTRIO   AZIE

seared white tuna roll topped with ground daikon-radish ponzu sauce.

 E3 ®57 115 CYRIL MAGNIN ST.
415-421-2101

LE COLONIAL *ROMANTIC • VIETNAMESE $$$*
With its tall shuttered windows, palm fronds, and whirling fans, this "French Colonial-era" Vietnamese restaurant looks like the set of a Bogey film. Relax on rattan chairs in the salon or out on the verandah before delving into a menu full of flavorful, aromatic delicacies.

 D2 ®33 20 COSMO PL.
415-931-3600

MASA'S *ROMANTIC • FRENCH $$$*
Under the command of star chef Richard Reddington, Masa's continues its reign as the city's most indulgent restaurant. Assemble your own prix fixe menus from three courses, such as tender duck breast with caramelized pears or black bass with taragon emulsion. The elegant decor incorporates sumptuous fabrics, recessed spotlights, and a striking, hammered-bronze sculpture.

B4 ®10 648 BUSH ST.
415-989-7154

MICHAEL MINA *HOT SPOT • AMERICAN $$$*
Located in the legendary Westin St. Francis, chef/owner Michael Mina's elegant new eatery invites guests to explore different taste sensations by pairing the main ingredient with a trio of garnishes. The 85-seat restaurant is welcoming in warm celadon and ivory tones, created by renowned designer Barbara Barry.

D3 ®43 335 POWELL ST. (WESTIN ST. FRANCIS)
415-397-9222

PONZU *BUSINESS • ASIAN $$*
Seated around intimate tables, shoppers and theatergoers refuel on dishes that draw from all reaches of Asia, from Vietnamese beef carpaccio to tea-smoked salmon with oxtail. Exotic fish swim behind the large curved bar, where a hip crowd sips imaginative tropical drinks from voodoo-mask glasses.

E2 ®55 401 TAYLOR ST. (SERRANO HOTEL)
415-775-7979

POSTRIO   *HOT SPOT • FRENCH $$$*

Wolfgang Puck's brainchild is a perennial darling among critics.
Upstairs, the café's wood-burning oven is central to a casual menu.
Downstairs, the atmosphere steps up to the acclaim: Amid paintings by Rauschenberg and Rosenquist, convivial servers present a
daily changing selection of Asian- and Mediterranean-influenced
California cuisine.

 D2 **R**35   545 POST ST.
415-776-7825

MAP **2** CHINATOWN/FINANCIAL DISTRICT/SOMA

ACME CHOP HOUSE   *HOT SPOT • CALIFORNIA-AMERICAN $$*

Get your greasy dogs and garlic fries at the ballpark. If you're looking for a more substantial pre- or post-game meal, reserve a table at
ever-packed Acme. Chef Traci Des Jardins scores big with her commitment to locally farmed ingredients and sustainable seafood.

 E5 **R**68   24 WILLIE MAYS PLAZA
415-644-0240

ALFRED'S STEAK HOUSE   *BUSINESS • STEAK $$$*

A carnivore's delight, this 50-year-old mainstay serves 18 different
steak dishes hot off a mesquite grill. Alfred's uses only corn-fed
Angus beef, and each cut is aged up to four weeks to guarantee
tenderness. Vegetarians accompanying their red-meat-eating friends
can choose from a variety of pasta dishes.

 A3 **R**6   659 MERCHANT ST.
415-781-7058

AQUA   *BUSINESS • SEAFOOD $$$*

Ambient lighting, breathtaking art, and elaborate floral arrangements hint at Aqua's clientele of Financial District power brokers.
Meticulous seafood presentations arrive in audacious combinations,
like lobster pot pie and tapioca-crusted Thai snapper. Try one of the
tasting menus.

 A4 **R**10   252 CALIFORNIA ST.
415-956-9662

AZIE   *HOT SPOT • ASIAN $$$*

A few doors down from LuLu, this sister restaurant entices with
intense Asian flavors in a palatial setting. For an intimate tryst, the
shuttered booth tables offer seclusion and drama. After work, office
escapees fill the bar, slurping down oysters and glasses of wine.

MAP **2** D3 **R**52   826 FOLSOM ST.
415-538-0918

BACAR   *HOT SPOT • CALIFORNIA $$$*

Oenophiles may have trouble selecting from among the more than
1,000 bottles at Bacar (Latin for wine goblet). Don't fret: 100 alternating choices from the three-story "wine wall" are available to

BOULEVARD   FIFTH FLOOR

taste in two-ounce pours. Also exhaustive, the seasonal American menu is worth the mental anguish it imposes.

 MAP 2 D4 R 57 448 BRANNAN ST.
415-904-4100

BOULEVARD *HOT SPOT • CALIFORNIA-AMERICAN* $$$
Chef/owner Nancy Oakes's inspired California-American creations and impressive dining-room views of the bay keep patrons waiting weeks for a reservation. A bit more attainable is a seat at the bar, where you can count on the bistro menu to include Boulevard's most popular staples.

MAP 2 A5 R 18 1 MISSION ST.
415-543-6084

CIAO BELLA *QUICK BITES • ICE CREAM* $
With ice cream and sorbet flavors like wasabi, chili lime, malted milk ball, and saffron cardamom, Ciao Bella's retail outpost is, bar none, the most decadent and unusual ice cream experience in town.

 MAP 2 A5 R 13 1 FERRY PLAZA
415-834-9330

FIFTH FLOOR *HOT SPOT • CALIFORNIA-FRENCH* $$$
At the tony Hotel Palomar, celebrity chef Laurent Gras reinvents classic French fare in bold combinations like tuna foie gras and a duet of beef and lamb Wellington. The bar is a trendy after-work spot for guests of the hotel and locals alike.

MAP 2 C3 R 28 12 4TH ST. (HOTEL PALOMAR)
415-348-1555

HAWTHORNE LANE *ROMANTIC • CALIFORNIA-ASIAN* $$$
Located in a brick alley just off the busy SoMa thoroughfares, Hawthorne Lane is a gustatory oasis. Seated at the cherrywood bar, sample well-priced treats off the ample café menu. Or retire to the more formal dining room, where roasted lamb and rice noodle-stuffed yellowfin tuna await.

 MAP 2 C4 R 40 22 HAWTHORNE ST.
415-777-9779

HOUSE OF NANKING *QUICK BITES • CHINESE* $
Despite the snaking-line wait for a table and the brusque service once you're seated, hundreds flock daily to this tiny restaurant for

well-spiced, swell-priced Hunan and Cantonese dishes. Be sure to ask about the specials.

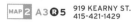 A3 **R5** 919 KEARNY ST.
415-421-1429

LE CHARM   *ROMANTIC • FRENCH $$*

On the rarity of a warm summer evening, this French bistro's leafy courtyard is a choice destination. The airy dining room, accented by cityscape photographs and contemporary jazz, more than suffices the rest of the year. Traditional recipes, quality ingredients, and a friendly staff make for a charming evening.

 D3 **R54** 315 5TH ST.
415-546-6128

MAYA   *BUSINESS • MEXICAN $$$*

Sister to the critically acclaimed Maya New York, this spacious eatery offers a sophisticated, gracious ambience in which to enjoy a world of options beyond the basic *taquería* chow. Sample sweet and spicy ceviche of mahi mahi and other gourmet Mexican dishes.

 C4 **R41** 303 2ND ST.
415-543-2928

MOMO'S   *BUSINESS • AMERICAN $$$*

Wood and leather, accentuated with reproduction antique prints and vintage San Francisco photos, generate Momo's warmth. Salads and pizzas lighten up the menu of comfort classics, like pork osso buco and herb-roasted chicken. The patio, opposite SBC Park, gets packed on game days but is a perfect place for brunch.

 D5 **R61** 760 2ND ST.
415-227-8660

ONE MARKET   *BUSINESS • CALIFORNIA-AMERICAN $$$*

One Market offers its corporate clientele a happy hour replete with familiar faces and martini perfection, followed by blissful pampering in the glossy wood dining room. The seasonal menu features locally grown American fare. Try shaved foie gras salad, Coloradi lamb "three ways," or grilled venison striploin.

 A5 **R17** 1 MARKET ST.
415-777-5577

OZUMO   *HOT SPOT • JAPANESE $$$*

Beautiful people are drawn to beautiful restaurants. And Ozumo, arguably one of the most exquisite restaurants in the city, is no exception. Masterfully prepared Japanese cuisine and creative, melt-in-your-mouth maki, nigiri, and sashimi balance the contemporary, waterfront setting.

MAP 2 A5 **R20** 161 STEUART ST.
415-882-1333

RESTAURANT LULU   *BUSINESS • MEDITERRANEAN-FRENCH $$$*

In this refurbished 1910 warehouse, a boisterous crowd sits beneath vaulted ceilings and skylights, sharing family-style plates of Provençal cuisine, including pizzas, pastas, and fresh shellfish.

THE SLANTED DOOR   YANK SING   THE BUBBLE LOUNGE

The wine bar features more than 70 wines by the glass and several themed flights, such as Napa Valley Reds.

MAP 2 D3 R 51   816 FOLSOM ST.
415-495-5775

RUBICON   *BUSINESS • CALIFORNIA-FRENCH* $$$

With names like De Niro, Lucas, and Williams behind it, the Rubicon offers a carefully orchestrated fusion of drama, quality, and pizzazz. In its loftlike setting (lots of cherrywood and brick), Financial District VIPs savor dishes like applewood-smoked duck, oxtail-crusted beef, and marinated yellowfin tuna.

MAP 2 A3 R 8   558 SACRAMENTO ST.
415-434-4100

THE SLANTED DOOR   *HOT SPOT • VIETNAMESE* $$

Since Charles Phan moved his family-run, nationally acclaimed Vietnamese restaurant into its new multimillion-dollar home, nearly every seat fills nightly. Appetizers such as local oysters and spicy green papaya salad are a good start to a memorable meal. His signature shaking beef is a bit pricier than before, but it's worth it.

MAP 2 A5 R 14   1 FERRY PLAZA
415-861-8032

TOWN HALL   *HOT SPOT • CALIFORNIA-AMERICAN* $$

Three talented guys, formerly of Postrio, poured a lot of love into opening the most-talked-about restaurant in town. Well-heeled locals pack this brick "town hall" for hobnobbing and deal-making over flavorful dishes like smoked chicken gumbo and roasted duck.

MAP 2 B5 R 26   342 HOWARD ST.
415-908-3900

XYZ   *HOT SPOT • CALIFORNIA-AMERICAN* $$$

With its posh bi-level setting and elegant banquettes, the W Hotel packs in the hippest of business travelers and locals. Three spreads of modern cuisine are served a day, and the cocktails flow all night at the hopping bar.

MAP 2 C4 R 39   181 3RD ST.
415-817-7836

YANK SING   *QUICK BITES • CHINESE* $

Yank Sing offers a superlative dim sum experience, with more than 60 varieties served daily, from minced squab lettuce cups to stuffed lotus leaves. The to-go counter supplies habit-forming combination dishes.

MAP **2** B5 **R** 25   101 SPEAR ST. (RINCON CENTER)
                    415-957-9300

MAP 3 NORTH BEACH/THE WATERFRONT

BIX *BUSINESS • AMERICAN* $$$
Bix's retro design and brick-alley location give it a speakeasy feel and old-time charm. You'll find tried-and-true classics like steak tartare and innovative new dishes like local, almond-crusted albacore tuna. The long bar specializes in all things shaken or stirred and is a popular spot for media types.

MAP **3** F5 **R** 37   56 GOLD ST.
                 415-433-6300

THE BUBBLE LOUNGE *AFTER HOURS • HORS D'OUEVRES* $$$
Chill with the beautiful people at this sexy sanctuary of immoderation, serving more than 300 kinds of champagne and sparkling wine. In the plush loveseats, spoil each other with fine cheeses, sashimi, truffles, caviar, and other such exquisite nibbles.

MAP **3** F5 **R** 40   714 MONTGOMERY ST.
                 415-434-4204

CAFFE MACARONI *ROMANTIC • ITALIAN* $$
The wait for a table at this legendary North Beach trattoria can seem endless. But it's well worth it for bountiful portions of gnocchi with gorgonzola sauce and braised lamb shank with rosemary over polenta. Just up the street, Macaroni Sciuè Sciuè (124 Columbus Ave.), a larger version of the original, serves lunch and dinner.

MAP **3** F5 **R** 38   59 COLUMBUS AVE.
                 415-956-9737

CAFFÉ TRIESTE *CAFÉ • ITALIAN* $
Widely recognized as the first espresso coffeehouse on the West Coast, family-owned Caffé Trieste first opened its doors in 1956. Sip a cappuccino, munch Italian pastries, and enjoy Saturday afternoon concerts by the Giotta family at this treasured North Beach institution.

MAP **3** E4 **R** 26   601 VALLEJO ST.
                 415-392-6739

CALZONE'S *AFTER HOURS • ITALIAN* $$
Better known for its fun, sidewalk tables than for an exceptional menu, Calzone's garners a faithful North Beach following. Still, its well-rounded selection of time-honored Italian specialties, such as the namesake calzone baked in an almond wood-fired oven, fresh pastas, and seasonal bistro fare, are solid.

MAP **3** E4 **R** 25   430 COLUMBUS AVE.
                 415-397-3600

BREAD BOWLS

Back in 1849, a baker named Isidore Boudin mixed a dash of French technique with the standard sourdough recipe – and voilà! – what arose was the Original San Francisco Sourdough French Bread for which this city has grown famous. Boudin Bakeries eventually added a new twist to the tasty loaves – they were hollowed into bowls and filled to the brim with thick and creamy clam chowder. Today hordes come from all over the world to stroll along Fisherman's Wharf, either anxious to try one of those steaming hot "bread bowls" they've heard so much about, or craving the comfort-food creation they remember so fondly from years past. Regardless of whether you're an out-of-town bread bowl virgin or a repeat local customer, it's that winning combination of chock-full-of-clams chowder seeping into the crusty sides of the sourdough bowl that makes you sigh into your spoon, and say I Love San Francisco.

CLOWN ALLEY *QUICK BITES • AMERICAN* $
This circus-themed cafeteria is one of the city's oldest and most popular burger joints. At lunch, the otherworldly bacon cheeseburgers draw long lines of suits and briefcases from the Financial District. Dieters and vegetarians can be found sinking their teeth into eggplant or marinated tuna sandwiches.

MAP 3 F5 R39 42 COLUMBUS AVE.
415-421-2540

FOG CITY DINER *BUSINESS • AMERICAN* $$
This local landmark showcases a stainless-steel, neon-lit bar, known for its Barbados cosmopolitan. A relaxed mix of professionals and tourists enjoy California-style American eats – like Tombo tuna sloppy joes, mu shu pork burritos, and a long list of oysters – at deep booths and sidewalk tables.

MAP 3 C5 R17 1300 BATTERY ST.
415-982-2000

GLOBE *AFTER HOURS • CALIFORNIA-AMERICAN* $$
Open 'til 1 A.M. six nights a week, this SoHo-style eatery (plenty of metal and exposed brick) serves up fine wines and uncomplicated California-American eats to an urban-chic crowd. A rotating selection of creative crusty pizzas give Globe a subtle Italian twist.

MAP 3 E6 R35 290 PACIFIC AVE.
415-391-4132

ILUNA BASQUE *HOT SPOT • BASQUE* $$
Twenty-something chef Mattin Noblia might be young but he cooks with mature passion. Enjoy a medley of well-priced small plates, like salt cod served with *crostini,* lamb chops, and garlic shrimp soup,

FOG CITY DINER   ILUNA BASQUE

with a pitcher of chilled, fruit-filled sangria, in an inviting, window-walled setting.

 MAP 3 E3 R20   701 UNION ST.
415-402-0011

KOKKARI ESTIATORIO   *HOT SPOT • GREEK* $$$
In the Greek fishing village of Kokkari, wild game and seafood hold a special place in the local mythology. At Kokkari Estiatorio, patrons enjoy Mediterreanean delicacies made with fresh California ingredients, amid rustic elegance, feasting on such classic dishes as fried smelt and grilled lamb chops.

MAP 3 F6 R41   200 JACKSON ST.
415-981-0983

L'OSTERIA DEL FORNO   *QUICK BITES • ITALIAN* $$
"Diminutive" best describes this Columbus Avenue spot, from the space to the portions. So cuddle up and double up on inexpensive, authentic antipasti, like stuffed tomatoes and beef or salmon carpaccio. Other specialties include panini on homemade focaccia and the hands-down favorite: milk-braised roast pork. Cash only.

 MAP 3 E3 R21   519 COLUMBUS AVE.
415-982-1124

MOOSE'S   *BUSINESS • AMERICAN* $$$
Ed and Mary Etta Moose's watering hole is the place to schmooze with local politicians, performers, writers, and media moguls while listening to live jazz. But it's not all about the scene; the daily menu features nationally acclaimed traditional California-American fare with Italian and Mediterranean influences.

MAP 3 D3 R13   1652 STOCKTON ST.
415-989-7800

PIPERADE   *HOT SPOT • BASQUE* $$
Distinguished chef Gerald Hirigoyen's bona fide Basque restaurant has quickly become a favorite among epicures. Enjoy spicy seafood stews, fork-tender pork daube, and French favorites like crisp fries and foie gras in Piperade's refined yet festive brick and burgundy surrounds.

MAP 3 D5 R18   1015 BATTERY ST.
415-391-2555

ROSE PISTOLA *HOT SPOT • ITALIAN* $$

Hosting live jazz Thursday through Sunday, Rose Pistola's vibrant dining room centers around a blazing hearth, where a wood-fire oven turns out crisp pizzas and well-roasted meats. Served family-style, the daily menu features modern Italian entrées, as well as a comprehensive list of varietals.

 MAP 3 E3 ℞ 22   532 COLUMBUS AVE.
415-399-0499

MAP 4 | MARINA/COW HOLLOW/PACIFIC HEIGHTS

ANA MANDARA *HOT SPOT • VIETNAMESE* $$$

Inspired by an ancient love story, Ana Mandara is finally a reason to visit touristy Ghirardelli Square. A bevy of exotic drinks (like the Ha Long Blue, a potent citrus cooler blended with lychee juice) injects some fun into the upmarket menu of Vietnamese classics.

MAP 4 B6 ℞ 15   891 BEACH ST.
415-771-6800

ANTICA TRATTORIA *ROMANTIC • ITALIAN* $$

Antica's light and relaxing interior sets the stage for bold, rustic Italian flavors. Follow up the complimentary antipasti with a seductive mozzarella salad or carpaccio, before delving into braised duck atop pappardelle or smoky grilled lamb medallions.

 MAP 4 C6 ℞ 32   2400 POLK ST.
415-928-5797

A16 *HOT SPOT • ITALIAN* $$

Not your typical pizza place, A16 pays praise-worthy homage to Italy. Simple prosciutto-topped pies, pasta with broccoli *rabe*, well-prepared fish such as petrale sole or quail, and an affordable wine list keep this successful new venture in the limelight.

 MAP 4 C2 ℞ 24   2355 CHESTNUT ST.
415-771-2216

EASTSIDE WEST *BREAKFAST AND BRUNCH • AMERICAN* $$

Eastside West features comforting American fare (especially East Coast seafood) as well as a first-class raw bar. Fans of the cosmopolitan though low-pretense atmosphere also come for jazz and reggae music during tranquil Sunday brunch on the sidewalk.

MAP 4 C3 ℞ 28   3154 FILLMORE ST.
415-885-4000

ELLA'S *BREAKFAST AND BRUNCH • CALIFORNIA-AMERICAN* $

Known for its top-notch service and warm atmosphere, visitors and locals alike are hard-pressed to name a better brunch spot than Ella's. Daily scrambles, chicken hash, homemade breads, and freshly squeezed juices draw a crowd of casually clad regulars to its corner every weekend.

 MAP 4 F1 ℞ 61   500 PRESIDIO AVE.
415-441-5669

ANA MANDARA   GREENS

GARY DANKO   *HOT SPOT • CALIFORNIA-AMERICAN* $$$
For a truly unforgettable meal, indulge yourself with chef Danko's complex, and accordingly pricey, inventions. The three-, four-, and five-course tasting menus may include an edifying session with the cheese cart, a careful selection of wine pairings, and a tableside preparation of cherries flambé.

 MAP 4 B6 **R19**   800 NORTH POINT
415-749-2060

GREENS   *HOT SPOT • VEGETARIAN* $$
Using only organic produce and the finest ingredients available, chef Annie Somerville balances colors, flavors, and textures to create her all-veggie Mexican-, Mediterranean-, and American Southwest–influenced dishes. The to-go counter is a convenient and inexpensive option for enjoying world-class health food anytime.

 MAP 4 B4 **R11**   FORT MASON, BLDG. A
415-771-6222

THE GROVE   *QUICK BITES • CALIFORNIA* $
The Grove's dark wood interior, accented with colorful blossoms from the neighboring florist, provides an inviting space to grab a delicious made-to-order bite while enjoying the Chestnut Street shopping scene. This hot local favorite offers a wide selection of soups, salads, sandwiches, and pastas.

 MAP 4 C2 **R25**   2250 CHESTNUT ST.
415-474-4843

LA FOLIE   *ROMANTIC • FRENCH* $$$
French for "the madness," La Folie maintains a combination of excellence and understatement. The cozy interior counterbalances haute dishes like baked goat-cheese pastry, braised rabbit legs, and lobster risotto. Choose among three-, four-, and five-course menus, relax, and enjoy the parade of impressive plates.

 MAP 4 D6 **R42**   2316 POLK ST.
415-776-5577

MERENDA   *ROMANTIC • ITALIAN* $$
With strawberry-red walls, a mahogany bar, and only 15 tables, Merenda transports you straight to star chef Keith Luce's version of Italy. Choose among two, three, and four mix-and-match courses.

QUINCE   CITIZEN CAKE   JARDINIÈRE

Pastas are homemade; meats are braised tender; and a professional but personable wait staff will make you laugh.

 MAP 4 D4 **R40** 1809 UNION ST.
415-346-7373

QUINCE *HOT SPOT • ITALIAN-FRENCH $$$*
Chef Michael Tusk honed his skills at the almighty Chez Panisse, and you can taste it in every bite. Behind the buzz surrounding this latest power spot lies a passion for premium products, which combine to satisfy a guest list ranging from mayors and moms to young couples.

 MAP 4 F5 **R69** 1701 OCTAVIA ST.
415-775-8500

ROSE'S CAFE *BREAKFAST AND BRUNCH • CALIFORNIA-ITALIAN $*
Sip a chilled glass of sauvignon blanc on the sidewalk of this sunny upscale corner café. Seasonal organic omelets, thin breakfast pizza topped with sunny-side-up eggs and ham, or a bowl of corned beef hash with Yukon potatoes and poached eggs are served with a smile.

 MAP 4 D3 **R36** 2298 UNION ST.
415-775-2200

TABLESPOON *HOT SPOT • AMERICAN $$*
This cozy Polk Street spot has always housed popular restaurants. Its latest 47-seat incarnation, opened recently by a couple of local industry veterans, caters to a young, professional crowd. This comfortably hip hangout featuring a comprehensive menu of well-priced wines and meals ranging from pork to pasta.

 MAP 4 D6 **R46** 2209 POLK ST.
415-268-0140

YABBIE'S COASTAL KITCHEN *BUSINESS • SEAFOOD $$*
With its award-winning wine list, acclaimed menu, and urbane feel, Yabbie's is a cut above the typical Russian Hill haunt. Ocean-blue textured glass and whitewashed brick set the tone for seafood and raw-bar delicacies at this long-loved restaurant.

 MAP 4 D6 **R45** 2237 POLK ST.
415-474-4088

MAP 5 | CIVIC CENTER/HAYES VALLEY

ABSINTHE *AFTER HOURS • FRENCH $$*

This South of France–style brasserie pays homage to the exuberance of the bygone belle epoque. Classic French fare, such as crêpes and soufflés, share the spotlight with a vast assortment of American-influenced French-Italian dishes. Unfortunately, you won't find its mind-altering namesake among the bar's eclectic selection of spirits.

 MAP 5 D4 ℝ34   398 HAYES ST.
415-551-1590

ARLEQUIN *QUICK BITES • FRENCH-MEDITERRANEAN $*

From the folks who brought us Absinthe comes this lower-key sibling for the eat-and-run crowd. The light, enticing Provençal and Mediterranean fare is made to take away, to enjoy at the stand-up counter, or, more comfortably, on the sunny garden patio.

 MAP 5 D4 ℝ35   384 HAYES ST.
415-626-1211

CITIZEN CAKE *QUICK BITES • CALIFORNIA $$*

Elizabeth Falkner's pastries are as aesthetically beautiful as they are to-die-for delicious. Few realize, though, that the industrial-modern, window-walled café serves breakfast, lunch, and dinner, too. Its location and accommodating hours make Citizen Cake a perfect pre-opera supper or post-symphony dessert stop.

 MAP 5 D4 ℝ27   399 GROVE ST.
415-861-2228

INDIAN OVEN *BUSINESS • INDIAN $$*

This perennial best-of poll winner has a nice sit-down atmosphere and a straight-up menu full of traditional curries, appetizers, and varieties of fluffy naan. The spice level of some dishes can be adjusted, and believe them if they tell you that spicy will be too spicy.

 MAP 5 F3 ℝ64   223 FILLMORE ST.
415-626-1628

JARDINIÈRE *ROMANTIC • CALIFORNIA-FRENCH $$$*

Jardinière's cocktail-glass entrance gives way to one of the city's most opulent supper clubs, where proficient servers bear artistically arranged plates of California-French fare along with truly extraordinary desserts. Request one of the plush purple booths overlooking the illuminated, circular bar from the mezzanine.

 MAP 5 D4 ℝ26   300 GROVE ST.
415-861-5555

SUPPENKÜCHE *HOT SPOT • GERMAN $$*

This Hayes Valley *Wirtshaus* specializes in rare imported beers and hearty yet upscale Bavarian delicacies, served at candlelit, communal, wooden tables. Vegetarians should stick with appetizers, like potato soup and bread dumplings, while carnivores will delight in spätzle with oxtail stew and venison in red wine–plum sauce.

MAP 5 D3 ℝ22   525 LAGUNA ST.
415-252-9289

ZUNI CAFE *HOT SPOT • MEDITERRANEAN* $$$

The daily Mediterranean-influenced menu at this S.F. institution always has a few sparklers, the wildly popular roasted chicken on Tuscan bread salad among them. Order from a mile-long list of oysters at the bar, where an eclectic, hipster crowd samples from the extensive wine menu.

 E5 Ⓡ 59 1658 MARKET ST.
415-552-2522

MAP 6 | MISSION/CASTRO/NOE VALLEY

BISSAP BAOBAB *HOT SPOT • SENEGALESE* $

World music and the slight fragrance of ginger linger in the air of this hip Senegalese eatery. The simple menu features traditional dishes such as *mafe* (vegetables in peanut sauce on rice) and *casamance* (grilled sole in a lemon garlic mustard sauce) complemented by their popular homemade ginger cocktails.

 C4 Ⓡ 43 2323 MISSION ST.
415-826-9287

BOOGALOO'S *BREAKFAST AND BRUNCH* $

Loud and popular with locals, Boogaloo's is pure Mission – the morning after. Tattooed and pierced servers wait on an equally colorful crowd, and the dishes are a mix of breakfast standards and more unusual items, such as the sweet plantain cakes served with black beans.

 D4 Ⓡ 54 3296 22ND ST.
415-824-3211

CHARANGA *HOT SPOT • CARIBBEAN* $$

With its fashionable, sangria-swilling crowd, this Mission café practically guarantees a festive meal. The fabulous food – from thick fried plantains to spicy seafood stews – comes at a price, though: They don't take reservations, so be prepared to wait.

 C4 Ⓡ 45 2351 MISSION ST.
415-282-1813

DELFINA *HOT SPOT • ITALIAN* $$

Nationally acclaimed Delfina bases its nightly menu on the best local products currently available, delivering unfussy, farm-fresh California fare. Black-clad, often pierced or tattooed, servers bring a bit of the neighborhood, but none of the attitude, inside.

MAP 6 C3 Ⓡ 32 3621 18TH ST.
415-552-4055

FOREIGN CINEMA *HOT SPOT • CALIFORNIA-FRENCH* $$$

Retreat from the urban bustle for a leisurely brunch in this modern brasserie's generous courtyard oasis. At night, foreign classics, independent features, and animated shorts projected onto the patio's brick wall offer the perfect accompaniment to the California-French menu. But it is a restaurant at heart so don't expect surround-sound.

 D4 Ⓡ 51 2534 MISSION ST.
415-648-7600

BISSAP BAOBAB

DELFINA

HOME   *HOT SPOT • AMERICAN $$*
As the locus of the Castro dining scene, Home acheives star status
with delightful comfort food and that most important of all ingredients: location, location, location. The heated backyard patio is a fun
place to sip cocktails and snack on appetizers.

MAP 6   A3 ℞ 1   2100 MARKET ST.
415-503-0333

LAST SUPPER CLUB   *HOT SPOT • ITALIAN $$*
The same owners of the insanely popular Luna Park took their successful business formula and recently opened the Last Supper Club,
just a few blocks away. Affordable wines, tasty Italian fare, and a
vibrant crowd combine for a night of good fun.

MAP 6   D4 ℞ 56   1199 VALENCIA ST.
415-695-1199

LA TAQUERÍA   *QUICK BITES • MEXICAN $*
Connoisseurs know that rice has no business inside a burrito. Better
to stuff them with more *carne asada, carnitas,* or chorizo. A longtime Mission favorite, this mural-walled joint pulls in locals all day
and night for a fix of the good stuff.

MAP 6   E5 ℞ 64   2889 MISSION ST.
415-285-7117

LIMÓN   *HOT SPOT • PERUVIAN $$*
From dark hardwood floor to high lofted ceiling, this Peruvian
restaurant is filled with the warm aroma of spices wafting up from
flavorful dishes like shrimp ceviche and steak sauté. Low lighting,
lime-colored walls, and attentive servers create a stylish and welcoming atmosphere.

MAP 6   B4 ℞ 20   524 VALENCIA ST.
415-252-0918

LOVEJOY'S TEA ROOM   *BREAKFAST AND BRUNCH • HIGH TEA $$*
At Lovejoy's, traditional English high tea is served in a quaint and
casual setting. Antique tables and sofas, mismatched china, and
friendly service add to the cozy feeling. High tea comes with your
choice of tea sandwiches, spring greens, fresh scones, and a bottom-
less pot of tea.

MAP 6   E3 ℞ 63   1351 CHURCH ST.
415-648-5895

TAQUERÍA CANCÚN   CANVAS CAFÉ

LUNA PARK   *HOT SPOT • AMERICAN* $$
Once a butcher shop (vacant for nearly 30 years), Luna Park now
resembles a Left Bank brasserie, complete with Parisian streetlamps
and soaring windows that look out on Valencia's eclectic pedestrian
traffic. Try the goat-cheese fondue, *moules frites* (mussels and
french fries), and make-your-own s'mores for dessert.

 C4 Ⓡ34   694 VALENCIA ST.
415-553-8584

MECCA   *HOT SPOT • AMERICAN-ASIAN* $$$
A sprawling circular bar, candelabras, plush drapes, and cushy
booths make Mecca quite a cozy date spot, or the place to celebrate
with family and friends over seared scallops and spare ribs. Deejays
spin soulful tunes six nights a week and occasional live acts add to
the festivities.

 A3 Ⓡ2   2029 MARKET ST.
415-621-7000

PAULINE'S PIZZA   *ROMANTIC • ITALIAN* $$
Not your run-of-the-mill pizza parlor, Pauline's lavishes guests with
candlelight, white tablecloths, and accommodating service, all of
which warrant slightly higher prices. Quality ingredients, salads
tossed with organic greens, crisp thin crusts, and creative com-
binations (fennel, bacon, and fingerling potato, anyone?) position
Pauline's above the rest.

 A4 Ⓡ5   260 VALENCIA ST.
415-552-2050

SAVOR   *BREAKFAST AND BRUNCH • CALIFORNIA* $
Here's a brunch place to make a morning of. Lines are long, but
portions are huge and that patio table is hard to leave. Enjoy jam-
packed crêpes, healthy salads, and California-style frittatas stuffed
with goat cheese, chicken apple sausage, or grilled chicken.

 E2 Ⓡ61   3913 24TH ST.
415-282-0344

TAQUERÍA CANCÚN   *QUICK BITES • MEXICAN* $
This festive hole-in-the-wall appears at the top of many locals' best-
taquería lists. The food – from the burritos to the nachos – is all

delightfully spiced, and a jukebox of Spanish-language hits can add rhythm to your meal.

MAP 6 C4 R 38   2288 MISSION ST.
415-252-9560

TARTINE BAKERY   *CAFÉ • CALIFORNIA-FRENCH*   *$*

Pastry goddess Liz Prueitt can prepare a display case to send the most disciplined dieter into a tailspin. Fluffy lemon meringue, fruit-topped bread pudding, and decadent brownies beckon from beneath the glass. Come lunchtime, hipsters line up for fig brioche, *croque monsieurs,* and hot-pressed sandwiches on homemade bread.

MAP 6 C3 R 33   600 GUERRERO ST.
415-487-2600

TI COUZ   *HOT SPOT • FRENCH*   *$*

Write your name on the white board and enjoy a pear cider at the bar while you wait. Although savory Briton-style crêpes are Ti Couz's specialty, the dazzler is the large salade de marée. For dessert, share a sweet crêpe with bananas, Nutella, and ice cream.

MAP 6 B4 R 14   3108 16TH ST.
415-252-7373

MAP 7 | THE HAIGHT/INNER SUNSET/INNER RICHMOND

CANVAS CAFÉ   *CAFÉ*   *$*

This airy café-gallery offers surprisingly various food options, which include salads, cold and grilled sandwiches, pasta, and an excellent hummus plate. Open daily until at least midnight – to the delight of area students and the occasional night-owl professional – the space often features live performances at night.

MAP 7 E2 R 24   1200 9TH AVE.
415-504-0060

CHA CHA CHA   *HOT SPOT • CARIBBEAN*   *$$*

It's always chaotic inside this long-loved Caribbean tapas restaurant, where tables of rowdy diners swill pitchers of sangria while gobbling rounds of small, tasty dishes like jerk chicken, pork quesadillas, and fried plantains. Be prepared for a wait, they don't take reservations.

MAP 7 E4 R 28   1801 HAIGHT ST.
415-386-5758

EBISU   *HOT SPOT • JAPANESE*   *$$*

For more than 20 years, this brightly lit, unassuming Inner Sunset spot has been drawing crowds for its impeccably fresh, quality cuts of fish in basic and exotic rolls. Ebisu does not take reservations, so bring a book or a good conversationalist to pass the time.

MAP 7 E2 R 23   1283 9TH AVE.
415-566-1770

KABUTO SUSHI   *HOT SPOT • JAPANESE*   *$$*

Seats at this narrow, locally renowned neighborhood spot are always in demand. After the wait, guests savor wakame seaweed salad,

CALIFORNIA CUISINE

Marked by an interest in fusion, California cuisine has always integrated diverse cooking styles and fresh ingredients. Thanks to the birth of the local, organic movement and California cuisine-queen Alice Waters, the Bay Area has been on the culinary map since the 1960s. It's every chef's dream to be surrounded by bountiful farmland, dairies, and pastures that produce some of the best products in the country – from juicy red strawberries, flawless avocados, and plump artichokes to Hobbs bacon, Niman Ranch beef, and Fulton Valley chicken. Culinary academies might churn out many of the world's finest chefs, but it's the Bay Area location that both breeds and attracts some of the most talented toques in the country, including such masters as Roland Passot (**La Folie, p. 33**), Traci Des Jardins (**Acme Chop House, p. 25**), Gerald Hirigoyen (**Piperade, p. 31**), and Laurent Manrique (**Aqua, p. 25**).

slabs of incredibly smooth fish, masterfully prepared maki, a stunning sushi-and-sashimi combination dinner, and an eclectic menu of misos and side dishes.

 C1 R9   5121 GEARY BLVD.
415-752-5652

MEL'S DINER   *AFTER HOURS • AMERICAN* $
Late-night, grease-craving party-crawlers start pouring into Mel's retro-style diner post-2 A.M. Outfitted in paper hats and starched white shirts, the wait staff serves up oozing grilled-cheese sandwiches, fat burgers, french fries, and thick milkshakes. The SoMa location (801 Mission St., 415-227-4477) is close to the area's nightclubs.

 B4 R8   3355 GEARY BLVD.
415-387-2244

PARK CHOW   *QUICK BITES • AMERICAN* $
This bustling bistro serves hearty classics such as burgers and steaks, as well as a few Asian-inspired specialties. With its oversized fireplace and wooden beams, the environment is as inviting as the food. Considered one of the city's best bargains, Park Chow is a hands-down local favorite.

 E2 R25   1240 9TH AVE.
415-665-9912

PLUTOS   *QUICK BITES • AMERICAN* $
The concept is brilliant – and much needed – these days: *healthy* fast food. Design a lunch or dinner from the cafeteria-style spread of juicy carved meats, gourmet salad fixings, mashed potatoes, and

EBISU   Q

other yummy sides. It's great to-go, but more fun to grab a pint and take a seat.

 F2 R35   627 IRVING ST.
415-753-8867

Q   *QUICK BITES • AMERICAN* $
The perfect setting for a first date: young crowds, comfy booths, a colorful scene, and an eclectic, tasty, and affordable menu. Q has plenty of chicken, steak, fish, and salad options, plus simple starters like fried calamari to pair with a nice, well-priced bottle of pinot.

 B3 R6   225 CLEMENT ST.
415-752-2298

MAP 8 | GOLDEN GATE PARK

ANGELINA'S   *QUICK BITES • AMERICAN* $
Don't let the long line deter you – it just means that this little deli out in the avenues is worth the drive. Have a picnic on nearby Baker Beach with a made-to-order sandwich, stacked with only the freshest ingredients, and a salad, like the Asian or "All American" potato.

 A5 R3   6000 CALIFORNIA ST.
415-221-7801

CLIFF HOUSE   *ROMANTIC • AMERICAN* $$
This seaside landmark was recently restored to its original 1909 look. While the Cliff House might be celebrated more for its spectacular views – the seals on nearby Seal Rocks or the sunset over Ocean Beach – its classic fare, such as sautéed scallops or grilled cider-marinated pork chops, satisfies.

 B1 R7   1090 POINT LOBOS AVE.
415-386-3330

KHAN TOKE THAI HOUSE   *ROMANTIC • THAI* $$
Perhaps the city's most stately and romantic Thai restaurant, Khan Toke is still casual enough to entertain large, lively dinner parties. Slip (shoeless) into a candlelit, sunken booth and enjoy fresh, well-spiced

traditional specialties like green papaya salad, satay, garlic prawns, and plenty of curries.

MAP 8 B5 R 10 5937 GEARY BLVD.
415-668-6654

MARNEE THAI *QUICK BITES • THAI $*
Behind its typical storefront exterior, Marnee Thai cooks up some of the best Thai food in San Francisco, with a staff unhesitant to give frank advice about the menu – the corn cake appetizer is a must. The Inner Sunset location (1243 9th Ave., 415-731-9999) is very convenient to the park.

MAP 8 E5 R 18 2225 IRVING ST.
415-665-9500

PIZZETTA 211 *QUICK BITES • PIZZA $*
This cozy, closet-size space serves delicate, thin-crust pizzas with big flavor, accompanied by carafes of fine red wine and simple salads made with organic ingredients. On that infrequent warm evening when the fog disappears, score one of the mosaic-topped sidewalk tables.

MAP 8 A5 R 4 211 23RD AVE.
415-379-9880

SO *QUICK BITES • CHINESE $*
The portions are huge, the prices are cheap, and the dumplings are so good you'll order seconds. Enjoy oversized bowls of your favorite dishes, from spicy string beans to pork soup. B.Y.O.B. if you prefer, and settle into the Outer Sunset's latest hot spot until the fortune cookies arrive.

MAP 8 E5 R 17 2240 IRVING ST.
415-731-3143

TON KIANG *BREAKFAST AND BRUNCH • CHINESE $$*
You'll find a diverse mix of food lovers waiting outside this dim sum destination. The delicious servings of old stand-bys, like plump potstickers and shrimp-filled rice noodles, and more distinct options, like fried snow pea tips, come around on trays – not carts – in the generic strip mall restaurant-style space.

MAP 8 B5 R 11 5821 GEARY BLVD.
415-387-8273

NIGHTLIFE

Best wine selection: **HOTEL BIRON,** p. 49

Best patio: **EL RIO,** p. 51

Oldest S.F. bar: **THE SALOON,** p. 47

Best deejays: **PINK,** p. 51

Best beer selection: **TORONADO,** p. 50

Best martini in a jazz club: **BRUNO'S,** p. 51

Best poolside cocktail: **BAMBUDDHA LOUNGE,** p. 49

MAP 1 UNION SQUARE

HARRY DENTON'S STARLIGHT ROOM *DANCE CLUB*

Atop the Sir Francis Drake Hotel, this lounge hosts a well-dressed, somewhat older crowd. Enjoy sweeping downtown views while sipping cocktails and dancing to '80s hits or, on weekends, to jazz-funk band the Starlight Orchestra.

MAP 1 C3 Ⓝ18   450 POWELL ST.
415-395-8595

RED ROOM *LOUNGE*

Adjacent to the Commodore Hotel, this plush bar is awash in dark red hues – a fantastically romantic place to enjoy a quiet conversation (and a signature red martini) with your companion.

MAP 1 D1 Ⓝ31   827 SUTTER ST.
415-346-7666

RUBY SKYE *DANCE CLUB*

Formerly a 19th-century Victorian playhouse, this downtown nightclub is now one of the city's sleekest. The lighting and sound systems are unbeatable, and smokers can light up freely in a protected mezzanine lounge.

MAP 1 D3 Ⓝ42   420 MASON ST.
415-693-0777

THE TONGA ROOM *LOUNGE*

Expect rainstorms every half hour, a kitschy 1950s decor, an extensive (but pricey) happy-hour spread, and potent cocktails at this legendary tiki bar and longtime local favorite inside Nob Hill's famous Fairmont Hotel.

MAP 1 A2 Ⓝ1   950 MASON ST.
415-772-5278

TOP OF THE MARK *LOUNGE*

Arguably the finest spot for a 360-degree view of San Francisco, this famous lounge boasts a perch atop the 1926 Mark Hopkins Hotel. Be sure to dress up.

MAP 1 B2 Ⓝ6   1 NOB HILL
415-392-3434

TUNNEL TOP BAR *BAR*

Don't be fooled, the Tunnel Top is no dive, not since being classed up with nightly deejays, a free jukebox, a funky chandelier of old wine bottles, and a trendy, good-natured crowd.

MAP 1 B4 Ⓝ11   601 BUSH ST.
415-986-8900

RED ROOM   THE TONGA ROOM   DNA LOUNGE

 CHINATOWN/FINANCIAL DISTRICT/SOMA

BUTTER *BAR*
Order a corn dog or mac and cheese with your gin sour and party with the young, up-for-anything crowd at this unpretentious, post-modern techno bar inside a converted garage.

 F1 69   354 11TH ST.
415-863-5964

CAT CLUB *DANCE CLUB*
This dark, rock-and-roll nightclub consistently pulls in a tattooed bunch and, on Tuesdays, metal heads for live music night Lucifer's Hammer. New wavers can check out weekly dance party 1984.

 E2 64   1190 FOLSOM ST.
415-431-3332

DNA LOUNGE *DANCE CLUB*
Three bars, an affluent young crowd, live nightly Webcasts, and a state-of-the-art laser simulator place the high-tech DNA Lounge among the trendiest, most sophisticated clubs in town.

F2 70   375 11TH ST.
415-626-1409

END UP *DANCE CLUB*
Famous for its hedonistic, all-day T-Dance parties every Sunday, the rundown End Up embraces the seedier side of S.F. nightlife. The vibe's friendly, and the giant patio adds a nice touch. Open after hours.

 E3 65   401 6TH ST.
415-357-0827

GLAS KAT *DANCE CLUB*
A velvet rope greets you at this slightly upscale spot, but don't be put off. Inside, the Glas Kat offers a massive dance floor, a dance-friendly crowd, and multiple rooms for partying or kicking back.

 D4 56   520 4TH ST.
415-495-6620

HOTEL UTAH *MUSIC CLUB*

Intimate and cozy, this comfortably worn and absolutely charming bar hosts great live music nightly. Come early for a seat on the small but funky balcony.

MAP **2** D4 **Ⓝ55** 500 4TH ST.
415-546-6300

LI PO LOUNGE *BAR*

Step through the mysterious, cave-like entrance and you're immediately enveloped by the dark, somewhat shabby, yet comfortable surroundings of this Chinatown classic. Watch for secret deejay parties downstairs.

MAP **2** A3 **Ⓝ4** 916 GRANT AVE.
415-982-0072

MEZZANINE *DANCE CLUB*

This vast new club inside a renovated warehouse attracts a mixed gay and straight crowd focused on dancing. House beats dominate the top-notch sound system.

MAP **2** D2 **Ⓝ45** 444 JESSE ST.
415-625-8880

111 MINNA *LOUNGE*

A rotating selection of edgy artwork fills the walls of this hip downtown lounge and gallery. A favorite with the after-work crowd, it turns into a hot club with cool deejays as the night wears on.

MAP **2** C4 **Ⓝ36** 111 MINNA ST.
415-974-1719

330 RITCH ST. *DANCE CLUB*

Restaurant by day, stylish music and dance club by night, this hard-to-find venue (tucked away along a tiny SoMa alley) packs in the 20s and 30s set with fab parties like the weekly Popscene.

MAP **2** D5 **Ⓝ60** 330 RITCH ST.
415-541-9574

MAP **3** | NORTH BEACH/THE WATERFRONT

BIMBO'S 365 CLUB *MUSIC CLUB*

Founded in 1931, Bimbo's has long entertained San Francisco in classic cocktail style, from its plush booths and velvet curtains to a live music roster that's included Buck Owens, Spiritualized, and Cassandra Wilson.

MAP **3** C2 **Ⓝ7** 1025 COLUMBUS AVE.
415-474-0365

BLIND TIGER *DANCE CLUB*

Frosted-glass tables, dimly lit corners, and candlelit bar tops give Blind Tiger a New York sophistication unusual for a San Francisco deejay bar.

MAP **3** F3 **Ⓝ36** 787 BROADWAY
415-788-4020

BIMBO'S 365 CLUB   JAZZ AT PEARL'S

15 ROMOLO *BAR*
The alleyway entrance is a challenge to find, but through it is a chic, low-lit bar. A martini-glass drink seems the appropriate accessory to match the turquoise banquettes and dark wood.

 E4 **N29** 15 ROMOLO ST.
415-398-1359

JAZZ AT PEARL'S *MUSIC CLUB*
This elegant North Beach bar is an intimate, dependable spot for live jazz. The performers are mainly local veterans, but the quality and the setting are superb.

 E4 **N30** 256 COLUMBUS AVE.
415-291-8255

THE SALOON *BAR*
The oldest bar in San Francisco (dating from 1861) attracts both tourists and locals for hot and dirty blues in a friendly, laid-back atmosphere. Here's a slice of history you can live in.

 E4 **N28** 1232 GRANT AVE.
415-989-7666

SPECS *BAR*
This former speakeasy still retains the charisma that made it a favorite Beat hangout. The setting is a bit dingy, but the vibe is friendly and the space is full of character.

 E4 **N33** 250 COLUMBUS AVE. (12 WILLIAM SAROYAN PL.)
415-421-4112

TOSCA *BAR*
You never know who might drop by for a brandy cappuccino at this comfortable North Beach institution, a favorite of local film celebs. Expect an old-world experience, complete with opera on the jukebox.

 E4 **N34** 242 COLUMBUS AVE.
415-391-1244

VESUVIO *BAR*
Jack Kerouac loved Vesuvio, which is why it's probably North Beach's most famous saloon. This cozy, bi-level hideout is an easy place to spend the afternoon with a pint of Anchor Steam.

 E4 **N32** 255 COLUMBUS AVE.
415-362-3370

MAP 4 | MARINA/COW HOLLOW/PACIFIC HEIGHTS

BUENA VISTA CAFE *BAR*

This historic 1898 establishment claims to have introduced Irish coffee to America more than half a century ago and to this day makes a comfy stop when the fog's thick and chilly.

 B6 **18** 2765 HYDE ST.
415-474-5044

GREENS SPORTS BAR *BAR*

Be it March Madness or the NFL Playoffs, Greens makes a rowdy but friendly place to watch the game on one of its many television screens while nursing a pint (they sport 18 on tap).

 D6 **44** 2239 POLK ST.
415-775-4287

HIFI *DANCE CLUB*

Cosmopolitans are the drink of choice among the young, beautiful crowd at the Marina's only true dance club. Funky, colorful lighting and slick vinyl booths give it a modern feel.

 C3 **27** 2125 LOMBARD ST.
415-345-8663

THE LION'S PUB *BAR*

A mixed, young crowd swarms this fern-filled former gay bar for its inventive fruit cocktails (signature Greyhounds feature fresh-squeezed grapefruit juice). The cheese and fruit snacks are free and tasty.

 F2 **63** 2062 DIVISADERO ST.
415-567-6565

MATRIXFILLMORE *LOUNGE*

Once a hip 1960s space run by Jefferson Airplane's Marty Balin, this now ultra-chic cocktail lounge has a hopping singles scene. The decor, like the crowd, is refined and contemporary.

 D3 **34** 3138 FILLMORE ST.
415-563-4180

ROYAL OAK *BAR*

With its leafy decor, plush Victorian-esque couches, and low-volume music, this amiable watering hole is a great spot for congregating with friends.

 D6 **47** 2201 POLK ST.
415-928-2303

TONGUE & GROOVE *MUSIC CLUB*

This live music/deejay club has a dance floor, stage, and bar near the front and a room in back with cozy couches and a fireplace.

 C5 **31** 2513 VAN NESS AVE.
415-928-0404

TONGUE & GROOVE   BOOM BOOM ROOM

MAP 5 | CIVIC CENTER/HAYES VALLEY

BAMBUDDHA LOUNGE *LOUNGE*
Inside this tranquil Tenderloin lounge, an upscale crowd indulges
in fabulous snacks, sips Guavapolitans by an outdoor pool, and (on
weekends) shakes to hip house and other funky grooves.

 C5 **N15**   601 EDDY ST.
415-885-5088

BOOM BOOM ROOM *MUSIC CLUB*
Formerly owned by late blues legend John Lee Hooker, this onetime
speakeasy is still a San Francisco favorite for live blues and R&B. The
bar is simple, with red couches accommodating early arrivals.

 B2 **N7**   1601 FILLMORE ST.
415-673-8000

HOTEL BIRON *LOUNGE*
Relax with a glass of cabernet, a selection of cheeses, chocolates, or
a taste of caviar at this romantic, Parisian-style wine bar.

 E5 **N58**   45 ROSE ST.
415-703-0403

JADE BAR *LOUNGE*
A short walk from City Hall, this gorgeous bar frequently fills with a
trendy crowd. It boasts three floors plus its own waterfall.

 D4 **N23**   650 GOUGH ST.
415-869-1900

MARTUNI'S *BAR*
The piano bar in back attracts a fun-loving, mixed crowd for sing-
alongs fueled by irresistible martinis. Expect to battle for barstools,
though, on weekend nights.

 F4 **N65**   4 VALENCIA ST.
415-241-0205

NOC NOC *BAR*
Noc Noc's unremarkable facade belies the otherworldly 21st-century

MARTUNI'S   BRUNO'S

cave awaiting inside. Down-tempo electronica suits the mood at this
dark and wacky Lower Haight hideaway. Beer and wine only.

 MAP 5 F2 **N** 62   557 HAIGHT ST.
415-861-5811

RASSELAS *MUSIC CLUB*
This relaxed yet sophisticated bar is a great place to indulge in
some quality live jazz, blues, and Latin music. An evening menu of
Ethiopian cuisine adds international flavor to the experience.

 MAP 5 B2 **N** 10   1534 FILLMORE ST.
415-567-5010

RICKSHAW STOP *BAR*
Genuine rickshaws decorate the corners of this spacious, mellow,
and super-friendly club. Weekly events are an eclectic mix, from
deejays to live music to benefit parties.

 MAP 5 D5 **N** 49   155 FELL ST.
415-861-2011

TORONADO *BAR*
This dimly lit haven maintains one of the finest beer selections in
the nation, with a changing roster of several dozen microbrews on
tap, including many hard-to-find Belgian ales.

 MAP 5 F2 **N** 63   547 HAIGHT ST.
415-863-2276

MAP 6 | MISSION/CASTRO/NOE VALLEY

BEAUTY BAR *BAR*
Get a manicure with your martini at this retro chain bar with sisters
in N.Y.C. and L.A. The 1950s salon theme – old hairdryers, glittery
pink walls – pulls in a stylish crowd.

 MAP 6 C4 **N** 39   2299 MISSION ST.
415-285-0323

BLISS *LOUNGE*
An upscale, pretty, and often preppy crowd fills this super-sleek Noe

Valley bar, known for its classy cocktails. The cozy back room is perfect for an illicit rendezvous.

MAP 6 E2 N 59 4026 24TH ST.
415-826-6200

BRUNO'S *LOUNGE*
Rat Pack cool seeps from the speakers, the cocktail list, and the original vinyl booths of this former-Italian-restaurant-turned-jazz-club.

MAP 6 C4 N 46 2389 MISSION ST.
415-648-7701

CAFE DU NORD *MUSIC CLUB*
At this former speakeasy, you'll find a snazzy, romantic hideaway. The superb live-music lineup includes indie rock, jazz, and blues.

MAP 6 B2 N 7 2170 MARKET ST.
415-861-5016

DALVA *BAR*
Dalva is a small but sophisticated oasis in an ocean of overcrowded Mission hipster hangouts. You'll find dramatic high ceilings, modern paintings, and a jukebox stuffed with indie rock and electronica.

MAP 6 B4 N 17 3121 16TH ST.
415-252-7740

EL RIO *BAR*
The large backyard patio is a major draw at this popular Mission bar and music club. Sunday afternoon salsa parties are a blast, and Friday happy hour features free oysters.

MAP 6 F4 N 69 3158 MISSION ST.
415-282-3325

HUSH HUSH LOUNGE *BAR*
Attractive, easygoing crowds come to slug cheap beer after work or down killer *mojitos* at this small deejay bar.

MAP 6 A4 N 4 496 14TH ST.
415-241-9944

MAKE-OUT ROOM *MUSIC CLUB*
Equal parts after-work bar, music venue, and deejay parlor, this spacious Mission hangout is a longstanding favorite among locals.

MAP 6 D4 N 55 3225 22ND ST.
415-647-2888

PINK *LOUNGE*
Shabby chic meets hipster mod inside this romantic lounge hidden on a grungy Mission block. Fashionable patrons sip champagne and Pink Shot cocktails while grooving to world-class deejay beats.

MAP 6 B5 N 24 2925 16TH ST.
415-431-8889

12 GALAXIES *LIVE MUSIC VENUE*
Named after a line on a local eccentric's sign, 12 Galaxies provides ample space, and the second floor offers a balcony-like view. The bands tend to play rock, and the cheaper cover nights can be hit or miss.

MAP 6 D4 N 52 2565 MISSION ST.
415-970-9777

2202 OXYGEN BAR AND ORGANIC CAFÉ *LOUNGE*
If you don't buy an oxygen session, which requires you to stick short tubes up your nose, beer, wine, sake, and sushi are your intake alternatives at this deejay-spun, yet conversation-friendly lounge.

MAP 6 C4 Ⓝ 37   295 VALENCIA ST.
415-255-2102

ZEITGEIST *BAR*
Excellent draft beers, tasty barbecue plates, and a motorcycle-inclined crowd give Zeitgeist a punk-rock edge. This Mission favorite, though, endears itself to all sorts, thanks to its spacious garden.

MAP 6 A4 Ⓝ 3   199 VALENCIA ST.
415-255-7505

MAP 7 | THE HAIGHT/INNER SUNSET/INNER RICHMOND

CLUB DELUXE *BAR*
Pull up a stool at this dark, retro-style bar and order something classic. It's the perfect place to discover your inner Sinatra.

MAP 7 E5 Ⓝ 32   1511 HAIGHT ST.
415-552-6949

G BAR *LOUNGE*
Attached to the Laurel Inn, the chic G Bar offers intimate sophistication. A stylish crowd enjoys the modern decor and gas fireplace.

MAP 7 A5 Ⓝ 4   488 PRESIDIO AVE.
415-409-4227

THE PLOUGH AND STARS *PUB*
This spacious pub pours a fine Guinness and features live Irish music, bluegrass, and a weekly trivia contest. It's as close to Dublin as you'll get in San Francisco.

MAP 7 B3 Ⓝ 7   116 CLEMENT ST.
415-751-1122

MAP 8 | GOLDEN GATE PARK

BEACH CHALET BREWERY *BAR*
The restored Beach Chalet is now an attractive brewpub and restaurant. Directly across from Ocean Beach, you can sip a pale ale while watching the sunset. Check out the historic murals downstairs.

MAP 8 D1 Ⓝ 13   1000 GREAT HIGHWAY
415-386-8439

TRAD'R SAMS *BAR*
Although worn around the edges, this circa-1939 tiki bar delivers plenty of good fun when you're in the mood for a mai tai.

MAP 8 B5 Ⓝ 9   6150 GEARY BLVD.
415-221-0773

S SHOPS

Best spa: **KABUKI SPRINGS & SPA,** p. 64

Best people-watching spot: **FERRY BUILDING,** p. 57

Best place to buy romantic candles: **DIPTYQUE,** p. 54

Best women's boutique: **METIER,** p. 55

Best vintage store: **RAYON VERT,** p. 68

Best place to buy music: **AMOEBA MUSIC,** p. 69

Best local designer: **LOTTA JANSDOTTER,** p. 65

Best place to plan your next vacation:
GET LOST TRAVEL BOOKS AND MAPS, p. 64

Best place to indulge your fantasies: **GOOD VIBRATIONS,** p. 67

Most diverse shopping district: **HAYES VALLEY,** p. 64

MAP 1 | UNION SQUARE

ARGONAUT BOOK SHOP *BOOKS*
This unique family-run business was founded in 1941 and featured in Hitchcock's *Vertigo*; it specializes in the history of the West, with an emphasis on rare San Francisco and California books.

MAP 1 C1❺13 786 SUTTER ST.
415-474-9067

AU TOP COIFFURE *BEAUTY AND SPA*
At this little house of pampering, you can get everything from a new, star-style hairdo to a luxuriously relaxing facial. Special perks include a view of downtown from your salon chair.

MAP 1 C5❺24 305 GRANT AVE., 6TH FL.
415-693-9999

BRITEX FABRICS *GIFT AND HOME*
Four floors and counting, Britex is one of the world's great fabric stores. The well-informed, attentive staff can help you navigate the maze of cotton, silk, rayon, and wool, while offering keen advice.

MAP 1 D5❺49 146 GEARY ST.
415-392-2910

CAMPER *SHOES*
Spain's famous shoemakers, known for their spirited and artful creations, keep Camper supplied with leather sandals, loafers, and boots. Take a moment to view the impressive wall murals.

MAP 1 D5❺52 39 GRANT AVE.
415-296-1005

CANDELIER *GIFT AND HOME*
This fragrant shop stocks exquisitely crafted candles of all shapes and sizes to complement the decor, soothe the soul, or add a sensual touch to bedroom or bath.

MAP 1 D6❺53 33 MAIDEN LN.
415-989-8600

DAVID STEPHEN *CLOTHING*
This Maiden Lane classic retains the same European air as its fair address. For three decades, it has sold fine menswear, sportswear, and accessories the old-fashioned way: A master tailor on the premises oversees all alterations.

MAP 1 D5❺46 50 MAIDEN LN.
415-982-1611

DIPIETRO TODD *BEAUTY AND SPA*
Style is a serious matter at this 6,000-square-foot downtown salon, where a diverse clientele flocks for precision hairstyles, makeovers, and facials by unusually amiable professionals.

MAP 1 C5❺28 177 POST ST., 2ND FL.
415-397-0177

DIPTYQUE *GIFT AND HOME*
This famous French boutique – one of only two in the United States –

 BRITEX FABRICS DIPTYQUE GUMP'S

must have decided to open on Maiden Lane because it exuded a certain *je ne sais quoi*. The petite outfit carries an exquisite and fragrant selection of candles, soaps, teas, and more.

 MAP 1 **D5 ⑤ 47** 171 MAIDEN LN.
415-402-0600

GHURKA *ACCESSORIES*
Ghurka's must-have accessories include featherweight leather travel bags, handbags with decorative jeweled clasps, and a variety of chic trappings, from leather-trimmed golf-ball buckets to alligator frames.

MAP 1 **C5 ⑤ 26** 170 POST ST.
415-392-7267

GUMP'S *GIFT AND HOME*
Opened in 1861, Gump's is a San Francisco icon. The gilded East-meets-West emporium of exclusive, high-quality housewares also carries Asian, American, and European art objects, jewelry, and gifts.

MAP 1 **C5 ⑤ 29** 135 POST ST.
800-766-7628

LEVI'S *CLOTHING*
This gigantic fashion emporium offers incredible customization services, while featuring new music and emerging art – a truly interactive shopping experience.

 MAP 1 **C4 ⑤ 21** 300 POST ST.
415-501-0100

MARC JACOBS *CLOTHING*
The flagship of Louis Vuitton's retro-obsessed wunderkind beckons moneyed Maiden Lane patrons with haute outfits and multihued leather handbags. Want more? Stroll two blocks to LVMJ's grand Union Square bazaar.

MAP 1 **D5 ⑤ 48** 125 MAIDEN LN.
415-362-6500

METIER *CLOTHING*
Favoring sumptuously designed women's fashions, this upscale favorite oozes exclusivity. By limiting its stock to one piece in each size, Metier guarantees that your selection will always be unique.

 MAP 1 **C5 ⑤ 25** 355 SUTTER ST.
415-989-5395

UNION SQUARE   MA MAISON

PESARESI CERAMICS *GIFT AND HOME*
Pesaresi deals in imported Italian centerpieces, vases, hand-painted
ceramic dolls, wrought-iron and ceramic-tile-top tables, and other
fine collectibles, including many museum-quality pieces.

 C6 §30   50 POST ST., STE. 43
                              415-362-4570

UNION SQUARE *SHOPPING DISTRICT*
The nucleus of all major commercial shopping in San Francisco,
Union Square forever bustles with activity. Impressive shops surround the square on all sides (Maiden Lane is popular for upscale
boutiques), satisfying countless shopaholics.

 D4 §45   BORDERED BY POST, POWELL, STOCKTON, AND GEARY STS.

MAP 2 CHINATOWN/FINANCIAL DISTRICT/SOMA

ALEXANDER BOOK CO. *BOOKS*
This family-oriented bookshop sells a wide array of children's books
along with literary fiction, poetry, world studies, cookbooks, and, of
course, to stay au currant, all the new best-sellers.

 B4 §24   50 2ND ST.
                              415-495-2992

ARTROCK *GIFT AND HOME*
ArtRock is one of the world's largest dealers in rock-and-roll collectibles ranging from 1960s psychedelia to modern alternative art. It
often hosts exciting exhibitions in the store gallery.

 D3 §53   893 FOLSOM ST.
                              415-777-5736

BOOK PASSAGE *BOOKS*
This quaint bookstore is a perfect match for the renewed energy and
spirit of Ferry Building. In its sunny interior, you will find a wonderful
selection of cookbooks among countless literary classics.

 A5 §15   1 FERRY PLAZA, MARKETPLACE SHOP 42
                              415-835-1020

BORDERS *BOOKS AND MUSIC*
Regardless of what you're looking for, chances are Borders has it — a new cookbook, a great magazine selection, a chai latte, or even a date. The Union Square location (400 Post St., 415-399-1633) is very convenient to other commercial shopping activity.

 MAP 2 E5 **S** 67 200 KING ST.
415-357-9931

FERRY BUILDING *SHOPPING CENTER*
A favored destination among urbanites looking to grab a gourmet burger, shop for cheese, or gather with friends over coffee; the newly restored Ferry Building has quickly become irresistibly chic. Don't miss the weekend farmers market.

MAP 2 A5 **S** 16 1 FERRY BLDG.
415-291-3276

JEREMY'S *CLOTHING*
This stylish shop is a seductive den of imperfect designer threads. Its menswear collection, just a few rows from the silk cocktail dresses, is one of the best in town.

MAP 2 D5 **S** 58 2 SOUTH PARK AVE.
415-882-4929

MA MAISON *GIFT AND HOME*
Inspired by the home accent boutiques of Paris, the husband-and-wife team behind Ma Maison deals in unique pieces imported directly from French crafters.

MAP 2 D5 **S** 59 592 3RD ST.
415-777-5370

SAN FRANCISCO SHOPPING CENTRE *SHOPPING CENTER*
San Francisco's most popular mall offers all the quintessential standbys — Nordstrom, Bennetton, J.Crew — accessible via an unusual circular escalator system that seems to ascend endlessly.

MAP 2 C3 **S** 27 865 MARKET ST.
415-495-5656

STACEY'S BOOKSTORE *BOOKS*
This Financial District mainstay fills three luxurious floors with everything from travel books and classic literature to one of the best magazine sections in town. The monthly reading series consistently showcases top authors.

MAP 2 B4 **S** 23 581 MARKET ST.
415-421-4687

MAP 3 | NORTH BEACH/THE WATERFRONT

AB FITS *CLOTHING*
This cheeky shop beckons young, fashion-forward urbanites with merchandise from the latest underground European and Japanese designers. It also happens to be right where Grant Avenue starts to get interesting.

MAP 3 D4 **S** 14   1519 GRANT AVE.
415-982-5726

ALLA PRIMA *CLOTHING*
This eye-catching shop sells nothing but lingerie from the likes of Cosabella, La Perla, and Dolce & Gabbana. Pieces range from delicate and frilly to sturdy and functional. Hayes Valley boasts a second location.

MAP 3 E4 **S** 23   1420 GRANT AVE.
415-397-4077

BARNES & NOBLE BOOKSELLERS *BOOKS AND MUSIC*
This Fisherman's Wharf outpost is a reliable source for all things written and recorded – especially guides to the Bay Area and beyond – along with software, cappuccino, and excellent bargains.

MAP 3 C2 **S** 6   2550 TAYLOR ST.
415-292-6762

**CANNERY WINE CELLARS &
CALIFORNIA GOURMET MARKET** *GOURMET GOODIES*
The gargantuan wine and spirits emporium sits adjacent to its sister store, the California Gourmet Market. Between the two, you'll find imported and domestic liquors, collectible wine bottles, beers from around the world, and more.

MAP 3 B1 **S** 1   2801 LEAVENWORTH ST.
415-673-0400

CITY LIGHTS BOOKSTORE *BOOKS*
Renowned San Francisco poet Lawrence Ferlinghetti co-owns this legendary mecca for Beat literature enthusiasts and alternative culture fanatics. It contains aisle upon aisle of critical social theory, poetry, emerging fiction, dadaism, and surrealism.

MAP 3 E4 **S** 31   261 COLUMBUS AVE.
415-362-8193

MOLINARI DELICATESSEN *GOURMET GOODIES*
This North Beach legend makes five kinds of sausage, ravioli, and tortellini, in addition to stocking a lip-smacking array of imported Italian delicacies, cold salads, cheeses, marinades, and sandwich fixings.

MAP 3 E4 **S** 27   373 COLUMBUS AVE.
415-421-2337

CITY LIGHTS BOOKSTORE   BROWN EYED GIRL

MAP 4 | MARINA/COW HOLLOW/PACIFIC HEIGHTS

AMERICAN RAG CIE *CLOTHING AND SHOES*
The sister of L.A.'s Melrose boutique features one level of cutting-edge and vintage designer fashions as well as grungier, decade-spanning secondhand finds: everything from sweats to cigarette cases.

 MAP 4 F6 $ 72   1305 VAN NESS AVE.
415-474-5214

THE BAR *CLOTHING*
Sister store to Casbah (next door), this spacious shop carries the perfect accompaniment to your new shoe purchase. Find to-die-for outfits by any number of top American and European designers.

 MAP 4 F1 $ 60   340 PRESIDIO AVE.
415-409-4901

BENEFIT *BATH AND BEAUTY*
Sure, BeneFit's ultra-girlie cosmetics line is available at Macy's, but with atmospheric music, in-store waxing and facials, and a playful vibe, this flagship boutique is well worth the trip.

 MAP 4 F3 $ 64   2117 FILLMORE ST.
415-567-0242

BOULANGERIE BAY BREAD *GOURMET GOODIES*
This bakery keeps locals lined up for sinful French pastries and crusty, piping-hot breads made from imported, organic flour.

 MAP 4 F3 $ 66   2325 PINE ST.
415-440-0356

BROWN EYED GIRL *ACCESSORIES AND CLOTHING*
Resembling a woman's boudoir and housed in a converted Victorian, this treasure trove of classic fashion also carries home furnishings, beauty products, books, and stationery.

 MAP 4 E2 $ 51   2999 WASHINGTON ST.
415-409-0214

GOOD BYES   MOLTE COSE

BUILDERS BOOKSOURCE *BOOKS*
One of the city's best resources for architecture and design books, as well as reference materials, Builders Booksource also keeps its clients abreast of the San Francisco architecture and design scene.

 MAP 4 B6 **S 16** 900 NORTH POINT ST.
415-440-5773

CHESTNUT STREET *SHOPPING DISTRICT*
Located in the heart of the Marina, this shopping district is home to a wonderful combination of new and old. Lined with impressive art deco theaters, you'll also discover everything from yoga studios and spas to top-notch bakeries and clothing stores.

MAP 4 C1 **S 23**   CHESTNUT ST. BTWN. BAKER ST. AND VAN NESS AVE.

DESIGN WITHIN REACH *GIFT AND HOME*
True to its name, this showroom – one of the company's most popu-lar outposts – offers sophistication with a friendly touch. Browse the chic premises for items like Eames chairs and Nelson clocks.

 MAP 4 F4 **S 68** 1913 FILLMORE ST.
415-567-1236

CASBAH *ACCESSORIES AND SHOES*
Pacific Heights fashionistas depend on this little house of style for the latest runway styles in shoes and handbags from top designers, such as Jimmy Choo, Emma Hope, and Christian Louboutin.

 MAP 4 F1 **S 59** 344 PRESIDIO AVE.
415-409-1218

FILLMORE STREET *SHOPPING DISTRICT*
This vibrant shopping district is one of San Francisco's most fre-quented with its wide range of shops boasting a diverse array of goods – everything from fine papers and modern furniture to designer clothing and top-of-the-line petcare products.

 MAP 4 E3 **S 52**   FILMORE ST. BTWN. EDDY AND JACKSON STS.

GEORGE *GIFT AND HOME*
George carries a broad and original collection of design-conscious

products for pampered pets, from enamel ID tags to gourmet doggie treats and Cat Trip catnip toys.

MAP 4 F3 **$65** 2411 CALIFORNIA ST.
415-441-0564

GHIRADELLI CHOCOLATE SHOP *GOURMET GOODIES*

The aroma of dark, milk, sweet, and semisweet chocolate will lead you to this siren shop, located in Ghiradelli Square. Trouble is, its savory morsels may keep you from touring the rest of the square.

MAP 4 B6 **$17** 900 NORTH POINT ST.
415-775-5500

GIRL STUFF *ACCESSORIES AND JEWELRY*

Whether you're on your way to work, the beach, or out of town, this adorable boutique provides all the right accessories. It stocks a wide array of colorful handbags, jewelry, and more.

MAP 4 D6 **$43** 2255 POLK ST.
415-409-2426

GOOD BYES *VINTAGE AND ANTIQUES*

Opposing one another across tony Sacramento Street, these men's and women's consignment boutiques inherit illustrious labels like Prada, Chanel, and Gucci from the city's chicest closets.

MAP 4 F1 **$58** 3464 SACRAMENTO ST.
415-346-6388

MOLTE COSE *VINTAGE AND ANTIQUES*

Italian for "many things," Molte Cose stocks an engaging array of antiques, new and vintage clothing, uncommon gifts, and home accessories on what is perhaps Polk Street's most happening block.

MAP 4 D6 **$48** 2044 POLK ST.
415-921-5374

MUDPIE *KIDS STUFF*

Well-heeled little ones are groomed for greatness at this delightful Union Street purveyor of cute clothes, handmade layette accessories, unique gifts, toys, and books.

MAP 4 C5 **$30** 1694 UNION ST.
415-771-9262

POLK STREET *SHOPPING DISTRICT*

San Francisco's original gay mecca is now a dizzying combination of folks from the Civic Center, the Tenderloin, and Russian Hill. On this diverse strip, posh boutiques mingle with grungy bars and whimsical bookstores.

MAP 4 C6 **$33** POLK ST. BTWN. UNION AND CLAY STS.

SARAH SHAW *CLOTHING*

Sexy sundresses and demure twin sets face off in this relaxed space. The comfy couch offers a breather from auditioning looks by today's eminent and emerging designers.

MAP 4 F2 **$62** 3095 SACRAMENTO ST.
415-929-2990

SPA RADIANCE *BATH, BEAUTY, AND SPA*
This full-service day spa softens and rejuvenates using its own line
of homeopathic facial products and gentle, sweetly scented waxes
and creams.

MAP 4 D3 S38   3011 FILLMORE ST.
415-346-6281

UNION STREET *SHOPPING DISTRICT*
Catering to young professionals and families, Union Street is a virtu-
al mall with its range of specialty shops, florists, and upscale chains
like Banana Republic.

MAP 4 D3 S35   UNION ST. BTWN. GOUGH AND STEINER STS.

WORKSHOP *CLOTHING AND SHOES*
This discreet establishment woos San Francisco's serious power
shoppers with high-end labels, fine cashmere, and Italian shoes. Don't
forget the kids: Workshop also carries charming children's apparel.

MAP 4 D3 S37   2254 UNION ST.
415-561-9551

ZINC DETAILS *GIFT AND HOME*
From pillows and sake sets to lamps and wall clocks, every item
available at Zinc reflects the owners' fervor for strong, durable
materials transformed into objects that convey tranquility, adapt-
ability, and polish.

MAP 4 F4 S67   1905 FILLMORE ST.
415-776-2100

MAP 5 | CIVIC CENTER/HAYES VALLEY

AMPHORA WINE MERCHANT *GOURMET GOODIES*
Stocking 300–400 international selections, Amphora focuses on
small wineries and offers the chance to make new discoveries at
good prices. A varying assortment is featured at $15 and under.

MAP 5 D4 S35   384-A HAYES ST.
415-863-1104

BELL'OCCHIO *GIFT AND HOME*
Italian for "good eye," Bell'occhio offers rare embellishments from
specialized European ateliers. Handmade silk roses, antique ribbons,
French toiletries and fragrances, and other captivating baubles fill
the romantic space.

MAP 5 E5 S60   8 BRADY ST.
415-864-4048

BLOWN AWAY *BEAUTY*
Comfortable and without pretense, this undersized Lower Haight
salon serves an eclectic, urban clientele, who keep coming back for
quality coifs at reasonable prices.

MAP 5 F2 S61   583 HAIGHT ST.
415-861-7075

A CLEAN WELL-LIGHTED   FLAX ART & DESIGN
PLACE FOR BOOKS

BULO *SHOES*
Italian for hip, fresh, and attractive, Bulo claims two Hayes Valley
shoe stores (the men's store is at 437-A Hayes St.) catering to the
fashion- and quality-conscious foot fetishist.

MAP **5** D4 **S** 33   418 HAYES ST.
415-864-3244

BUU *ACCESSORIES AND JEWELRY*
Buu's serene ambience complements its lifestyle accoutrements. On
display are jewelry, bedding, candles, home accessories, and aroma-
therapy products made by Finnish, Japanese, and local designers.

MAP **5** D4 **S** 30   506 HAYES ST.
415-626-1503

A CLEAN WELL-LIGHTED PLACE FOR BOOKS *BOOKS*
This local independent prides itself on a knowledgeable staff of
career booksellers and hosts several weekly events featuring diverse
locally and nationally renowned writers.

MAP **5** C5 **S** 16   601 VAN NESS AVE.
415-441-6670

DISH CLOTHING *CLOTHING*
While sure to set you back several hundred dollars, splurging at this
minimalist boutique will refresh your wardrobe with the season's
essential items. You'll find au courant jeans, blouses, sweaters,
trench coats, and jewelry.

MAP **5** D4 **S** 36   541 HAYES ST.
415-252-5997

FLAX ART & DESIGN *GIFT AND HOME*
Considered *the* place for fine paper, stationery, art supplies, and cus-
tom albums, this oversized art store offers leisurely browsing opportunities after lunch at the Zuni Cafe, located across the street.

MAP **5** E4 **S** 55   1699 MARKET ST.
415-552-2355

FLIGHT 001 *ACCESSORIES*
Named after Pan Am's original round-the-world flight, this shop
furnishes sophisticated urbanites with stylish but functional travel

GET LOST TRAVEL
BOOKS AND MAPS

KABUKI SPRINGS & SPA

accessories, such as water-resistant toiletry bags, hard-to-find travel guides, and other paraphernalia.

 MAP 5 D4 S 37   525 HAYES ST.
415-487-1001

FRIEND *GIFT AND HOME*
A haven for all things designer, this corner shop favors locally and internationally renowned artists specializing in the funkiest of furniture, housewares, rings, stationery, and watches. A helpful staff keeps Friend true to its name.

MAP 5 D4 S 39   401 HAYES ST.
415-552-1717

GET LOST TRAVEL BOOKS AND MAPS *BOOKS*
Hands-down the best place for travel guides, maps, and accoutrements (you never know when a compass will come in handy), Get Lost also carries an extensive selection of travel literature.

MAP 5 F4 S 67   1825 MARKET ST.
415-437-0529

HASEENA *CLOTHING*
Feminine types feel at home amid all these flowery, flowing dresses, sheer blouses, cute handbags, and antique-style trinkets. With reasonable prices and a diverse selection, most shoppers don't leave the store empty handed.

MAP 5 D4 S 29   526 HAYES ST.
415-252-1104

HAYES VALLEY *SHOPPING DISTRICT*
Although petite, this shopping district offers a superb range of exclusive boutiques. Whether in the market for a designer couch, French candles, or fine cashmere, you're bound to find it here.

MAP 5 E2 S 52   HAYES ST. BTWN. GOUGH AND STEINER STS.

KABUKI SPRINGS & SPA *SPA*
Boasting more than 18 treatment rooms, a hot pool, and a wet and dry sauna, this Japantown sanctuary offers an endless array of services that are sure to leave you feeling like you've reached nirvana.

MAP 5 B2 S 8   1750 GEARY BLVD.
415-922-6000

LOTTA JANSDOTTER *GIFT AND HOME*
Behind its petite storefront, this inspirational atelier keeps a bountiful stock of exquisitely crafted stationery, notebooks, linens, aprons, pottery, clothing, and more.

MAP 5 A6 ⑤5 864 POST ST.
415-409-1457

MANIFESTO *CLOTHING*
Manifesto offers 1950s- and 1960s-inspired designs created by owners Sarah Franko and Suzanne Castillo. For men: textured, button-down shirts. For women: curvaceously cut rayon dresses.

MAP 5 D4 ⑤32 514 OCTAVIA ST.
415-431-4778

OXENROSE *BEAUTY*
Edgy young things swear by Oxenrose for avant-garde haircuts and bright, often extreme, color. A coffee bar on the premises ups the tempo, as does the house music.

MAP 5 D4 ⑤31 500 HAYES ST.
415-252-9723

PAOLO *SHOES*
Paolo Iantorno's Italian piazza-style boutique showcases his collection of handcrafted shoes, for which all leathers and textiles are conscientiously selected and then inspected to ensure top quality.

MAP 5 B2 ⑤6 1971 SUTTER ST.
415-885-5701

RE:FRESH *BATH, BEAUTY, AND SPA*
At this generous spa, more than 30 treatments – many using citrus or herbs – help you "re:new" and "re:juvenate," as do exotic teas, soft robes, and complimentary steam and sauna sessions.

MAP 5 B5 ⑤13 1130 POST ST.
415-563-2316

SHEHE *CLOTHING*
Urban trendsetters find cutting-edge clothing and accessories for men and women at Shehe. Plenty of Italian and New York lines mingle with a private-label collection.

MAP 5 E3 ⑤53 501 FELL ST.
415-552-4030

STITCH *CLOTHING*
Taking the term "stitch and bitch" to a whole new level, this little atelier houses a seamstress collective, who displays and sells inexpensive T-shirts, bags, skirts, and jeans in an inviting, casual environment.

MAP 5 E4 ⑤54 182 GOUGH ST.
415-431-3739

SUGAR AT M² *BEAUTY, GIFT, AND HOME*
In an arresting, stark-white setting, Sugar at M² is both a retail space and hair salon. Its ever-changing living room displays purchasable high-end wares from up-and-coming designers.

MAP 5 A6 ⑤4 912 SUTTER ST.
415-409-7842, 415-474-6262

VER UNICA *VINTAGE AND ANTIQUES*

This welcoming vintage boutique lays claim to a high-quality assem-
blage of men's and women's clothing and accessories dating from the
1910s to the present, with new locally designed, retro-inspired looks.

 D4 **⑤38** 437-B HAYES ST.
415-431-0688

MAP 6 | MISSION/CASTRO/NOE VALLEY

ADS HATS *ACCESSORIES*

No matter the style, shape, or craze, if it's a hat you're after, Ads
Hats is the place for you. This millinery powerhouse offers both variety and endless hours of fun.

 C4 **⑤36** 758 VALENCIA ST.
415-255-2787

AQUARIUS RECORDS *MUSIC*

The oldest independent record store in town, Aquarius makes music
collectors, from amateurs to aficionados, feel at home with its welcoming vibe, 50-plus CD listening stations, and specialized selections
of cult and experimental genres.

 D4 **⑤50** 1055 VALENCIA ST.
415-647-2272

BOOKS INC. OUTLET STORE *BOOKS*

This branch of the West Coast's oldest independent bookseller
peddles bargains for the coffee table, the cook, the child, and the
computer geek – along with last year's best-sellers.

 B2 **⑤11** 160 FOLSOM ST.
415-442-4830

CLIFF'S VARIETY *GIFT AND HOME*

Cliff's is no ordinary hardware store, though it does carry jigsaws
and wrenches. Check out its delightful array of bric-a-brac, from toys
to wigs and lava lamps.

 C2 **⑤30** 479 CASTRO ST.
415-431-5365

COTTAGE INDUSTRY *GIFT AND HOME*

Cottage Industry overflows with exotic treasures from all over the
world: masks, statues, drums, clothing, perfume bottles, painted can-
vases, beaded jewelry, and a hint of spicy incense.

 E2 **⑤58** 4068 24TH ST.
415-821-2465

DEMA *CLOTHING*

At designer Dema Grim's quirky boutique, you'll find a range of cotton goodies, from Three Dots to Orla Kiely, as well as fine cashmere
blends and silk dresses.

 D4 **⑤48** 1038 VALENCIA ST.
415-206-0500

READ AND DRINK

According to a recent study released by the Bureau of Labor Statistics, the average San Franciscan spends more on alcohol and books than residents of any other city in the United States. Also ranking highest in household income, San Franciscans may spend more because they earn more. But who can resist the great assortment of bookstores and choices of wine and spirits in this foggy city? Join in the Frisco addiction and stop in **City Lights Bookstore (p. 58), A Clean Well-lighted Place for Books (p. 63),** or **Green Apple Books & Music (p. 70)** for a typical San Francisco book fix; and mingle with the booze snobs at **Cannery Wine Cellars (p. 58)** and **Amphora Wine Merchant (p. 62)** — both have overwhelmingly huge wine and spirits selections.

826 VALENCIA *BOOKS*
Author Dave Eggers's tongue-in-cheek storefront doubles as a pirate supply shop and youth literacy center. While you'll find plenty of pirate booty here, you'll also find a good stock of literary magazines and books.

 C4 $40 826 VALENCIA ST.
415-642-5905

GALLERY OF JEWELS *ACCESSORIES AND JEWELRY*
The Gallery showcases limited-edition pieces mainly by local artists, along with an impressive vintage collection. Silver, gold, and platinum items range from delicate to bold.

 E2 $57 4089 24TH ST.
415-285-0626

GLOBAL EXCHANGE *GIFT AND HOME*
Spicily scented and draped with vivid, shimmering fabrics, Global Exchange is guilt-free shopping at its best. Most crafts, furnishings, and clothing are bought directly from artisans in developing countries.

 E2 $60 4018 24TH ST.
415-648-8068

GOOD VIBRATIONS/OPEN ENTERPRISES, INC. *GIFT AND HOME*
Worker-owned and woman-centric, this cooperative is brimming with electric relationship savers, erotica, and adult videos. Whether you're looking for toys or ploys, the helpful staff can point you in a blissful direction.

 B4 $22 603 VALENCIA ST.
415-522-5460

HARVEST RANCH MARKET *GOURMET GOODIES*
In addition to the sprawling soup-and-salad bar, bakery, deli, and

SUNHEE MOON   THERAPY   BEHIND THE POST OFFICE

organic produce sections, Harvest Ranch stocks hard-to-find gourmet grocery products, from freshly baked local breads to Vegemite.

MAP 6 B2 S10   2285 MARKET ST.
415-626-0805

LUCCA RAVIOLI CO. *GOURMET GOODIES*
Under a ceiling map of Italy sit shelves of fine imported wines, oils,
vinegars, fresh pastas, and tinned fish. Take a number for perfect
marinara, Parma prosciutto, and marinated olives.

MAP 6 D4 S53   1100 VALENCIA ST.
415-647-5581

MODERN TIMES *BOOKS*
This Mission district classic is the sort of bookstore that invites
hours of lingering among its various sections of new books, with
a large selection of gay and lesbian, Latino, and poetry titles. The
comfy, overstuffed chairs make you feel right at home.

MAP 6 C4 S41   888 VALENCIA ST.
415-282-9246

RAYON VERT *GIFT AND HOME*
Originally opened as owner Kelly Kornegay's flower studio, Rayon
Vert retains the charm (and fragrance) of a florist shop. Enjoy the
ambience while browsing captivating paper goods, antique maps,
and quirky wall decorations.

MAP 6 B4 S15   3187 16TH ST.
415-861-3516

ROLO *CLOTHING AND SHOES*
Rolo powers the local elite designer-clothing market at three locales,
including one Castro men's shop (complete with an in-store Kiehl's
boutique), a downtown store (1235 Howard St.) and a SoMa outlet
(1301 Howard St.).

MAP 6 B2 S9   2351 MARKET ST.
415-431-4545

SUNHEE MOON *CLOTHING*
Sunhee's own line of classic separates with a twist fits petite gals
perfectly. Her boutique also carries jewelry, bags, sunglasses, and
other accessories from local designers.

MAP 6 B4 S16   3167 16TH ST.
415-355-1800

THERAPY *GIFT AND HOME*
Therapy surpasses the nearby competition with its well-priced mix of recycled and new retro-style furniture, accessories, clothing, and goofy gifts.

MAP **6** B4 **⑤** 21 545 VALENCIA ST.
415-861-6213

24TH STREET *SHOPPING DISTRICT*
This lively thoroughfare caters to a more settled set: mothers with strollers, women after designer boutiques, and the professional Sunday brunch crowd. Browse flower shops, children's clothing stores, and accessory-heavy shops.

MAP **6** E2 **⑤** 62 24TH ST. BTWN SANCHEZ AND CASTRO STS·

VALENCIA STREET *SHOPPING DISTRICT*
As eclectic as the Mission district itself, this popular thoroughfare runs the gamut, from great books to Indian ice cream and taxidermy. Shop owners aren't afraid to go out on a limb in this edgy neighborhood.

MAP **6** B4 **⑤** 19 VALENCIA ST. BTWN. 16TH AND 24TH STS·

MAP 7 | THE HAIGHT/INNER SUNSET/INNER RICHMOND

AMOEBA MUSIC *MUSIC*
Located in an old bowling alley, this larger-than-life record store promotes every type of music imaginable. Amoeba's staff, many of whom are musicians themselves, are among the most knowledgeable in the business.

MAP **7** E4 **⑤** 27 1855 HAIGHT ST.
415-831-1200

BEHIND THE POST OFFICE *CLOTHING*
Focusing on obscure European designers and hard-to-find New York and Los Angeles labels, this boutique stands out against its grungier neighbors. Seven jeans, Velvet tees, and Orla Kiely bags are in hot supply here.

MAP **7** D5 **⑤** 18 1510 HAIGHT ST.
415-861-2507

BOOKSMITH *BOOKS*
This award-winning Haight Street bookstore boasts a helpful and informed staff, a fabulous magazine collection, and Northern California's preeminent calendar of readings by internationally renowned authors.

MAP **7** D5 **⑤** 15 1644 HAIGHT ST.
415-863-8688

EGG *GIFT AND HOME*
Beyond the eponymous birds' eggs housed in glass jars is a wide array of both the beautiful and quirky, from jewelry to letter-pressed stationery and Asian ceramics.

MAP **7** E5 **⑤** 33 85 CARL ST.
415-564-2248

GAMESCAPE *KIDS STUFF*
Having grown with the industry, this former chess and war-games shop now stocks almost every game imaginable — including, of course, computer and board games — from all over the world.

MAP **7** D6 S 21   333 DIVISADERO ST.
415-621-4263

GREEN APPLE BOOKS & MUSIC *BOOKS AND MUSIC*
Depicting rows full of eclectic folks milling about a vast assortment of new and used titles, the mural above Green Apple's sign accurately portrays the scene behind its timeworn doors.

MAP **7** B2 S 5   506 CLEMENT ST.
415-387-2272

HAIGHT STREET *SHOPPING DISTRICT*
Haight-Ashbury can't seem to shake its peace- and psychedelic drug-loving past. While this stretch caters to all kinds (there's even a Gap), you'll still find plenty of head shops, tie-dyes, and punks bumming for change.

MAP **7** D6 S 19   HAIGHT ST. BTWN. BAKER AND STANYAN STS.

JOE PYE *CLOTHING*
Owner Juliana Beach stocks the shelves here with designer duds that could make any fashion-forward woman giddy. Check out the boutique's digs — they were once home to the Church of John Coltrane.

MAP **7** D6 S 20   351 DIVISADERO ST.
415-355-1051

KIDS ONLY *KIDS STUFF*
Little ones can sport some Haight-Ashbury attire thanks to this purveyor of hand-tie-dyed clothing for infants through teens. Kids Only also sells unusual hats, toys, and puppets.

MAP **7** D5 S 16   1608 HAIGHT ST.
415-552-5445

KWEEJIBO CLOTHING CO. *CLOTHING*
All of Kweejibo's locally designed, retro-inspired men's shirts come in silks, linens, and synthetics that induce a tactile response. Twenty percent of their price goes to civic and arts organizations.

MAP **7** D5 S 17   1580 HAIGHT ST.
415-552-3555

SUSAN *CLOTHING*
Susan's Presidio Heights boutique offers the consummate European and Japanese designer collections along with a professional, gracious staff to help develop your style.

MAP **7** A4 S 3   3685 SACRAMENTO ST.
415-922-3685

WASTELAND *CLOTHING AND SHOES*
Originally a vaudeville theater, this capacious Haight Street shop has a traffic-stopping art nouveau facade, a distinctive assortment of vintage hippie/rockstar threads, and a glamour-punk staff.

MAP **7** D4 S 14   1660 HAIGHT ST.
415-863-3150

A ARTS AND LEISURE

MUSEUMS AND GALLERIES

MAP 1 | UNION SQUARE

49 GEARY
Ground zero for the San Francisco art scene, 49 Geary is home to many of the city's finest galleries. It also hosts the ever-popular First Thursdays, a monthly art walk that takes place the first Thursday of every month.

MAP 1 D5 ⚓ 50   49 GEARY ST.

FRAENKEL GALLERY
This esteemed photography gallery offers showings by renowned 20th-century photographers, such as Diane Arbus, Nan Goldin, and Garry Winogrand, in addition to countless other well-known modernists.

MAP 1 D5 ⚓ 51   49 GEARY ST., STE. 450
415-981-2661

MEYEROVICH GALLERY
One of the city's oldest and best-regarded galleries, Meyerovich brings the estates of Lichtenstein, Chagall, and Picasso within easy reach of lunchers on Maiden Lane.

MAP 1 C5 ⚓ 27   251 POST ST., 4TH FL.
415-421-7171

MAP 2 | CHINATOWN/FINANCIAL DISTRICT/SOMA

CALIFORNIA ACADEMY OF SCIENCES
A consortium of three institutions — Natural History Museum, Morrison Planetarium, and Steinhart Aquarium — the academy will remain in its temporary location until it reopens in 2008 following restoration and redesign by architect Renzo Piano.

MAP 2 D3 ⚓ 48   875 HOWARD ST.
415-750-7145

CALIFORNIA HISTORICAL SOCIETY
This small museum celebrates California history in imaginative and often startling ways — a past exhibit featured citrus-label art — and often mines its own archives, stored in a vault under the building.

MAP 2 C3 ⚓ 30   678 MISSION ST.
415-357-1848

MEYEROVICH GALLERY

CALIFORNIA ACADEMY OF SCIENCES

CARTOON ART MUSEUM

One of only two museums devoted to cartoon art in the United States, this one was founded by genre enthusiasts in 1984 and got a helping hand from Peanuts creator, the late Charles M. Schulz.

 C4 ⓐ35   655 MISSION ST.
415-227-8666

CHINESE HISTORICAL SOCIETY OF AMERICA

The society showcases some 50,000 items documenting Chinese American history, including the original dragon's head from San Francisco's first Chinese New Year Parade.

 A2 ⓐ3   965 CLAY ST.
415-391-1188

THE CONTEMPORARY JEWISH MUSEUM

Featuring a range of exhibits related to Jewish culture and life, this tiny musuem will increase in size when it moves in 2007 to its new Mission Street location designed by world-famous architect Daniel Libeskind.

 A5 ⓐ19   121 STEUART ST.
415-591-8800

LIMN GALLERY

Nestled in the back of the LIMN showroom, this sophisticated gallery is where you will find exhibits focused on the fusion between art and design. Be sure to stroll around the showroom first for added inspiration.

 E5 ⓐ66   292 TOWNSEND ST.
415-977-1300

THE LUGGAGE STORE

You won't find luggage at the top of this flight of stairs, but you will find one of the city's original grassroots spaces, devoted solely to the work of local artists, both emerging and prominent.

 D2 ⓐ44   1007 MARKET ST.
415-255-5971

NATURAL HISTORY MUSEUM

If displays covering eons of natural history – from the Ice Age to the

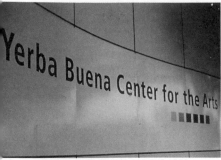

YERBA BUENA CENTER FOR THE ARTS
GALLERIES

MUSÉE MÉCANIQUE

space age – become overwhelming, the museum's 150-plus original *Far Side* comics will help to put everything in perspective.

MAP 2 D3 ⓐ49 875 HOWARD ST.
415-750-7145

SAN FRANCISCO CABLE CAR BARN MUSEUM
Giant wheels at this working powerhouse drive the city's cable car network. Inside, learn how it all works and pick up a little empathy for the gripmen.

MAP 2 A2 ⓐ1 1201 MASON ST.
415-474-1887

SFMOMA
See SIGHTS, p. 5.

MAP 2 C4 ✪38 151 3RD ST.
415-357-4000

SOMARTS
One of the city's older art galleries, SomArts can be found tucked under the freeway near the city's popular design and flower marts. This 30,000-square-foot warehouse has a series of rotating exhibits, a theater, and printmaking and ceramics studios.

MAP 2 F3 ⓐ71 934 BRANNAN ST.
415-552-2131

STEINHART AQUARIUM
Sharks, barracuda, and thousands of other water creatures occupy tanks replicating natural ecosystems. Tactile learners can touch anemones, hermit crabs, and urchins at a hands-on exhibit.

MAP 2 D3 ⓐ50 875 HOWARD ST.
415-750-7145

VARNISH FINE ART
At this local gallery, enjoy a wide range of contemporary works by great masters and emerging local talent, while sipping a fantastic selection of California wines poured by the gregarious owners.

MAP 2 C4 ⓐ37 77 NATOMA ST.
415-222-6131

WELLS FARGO HISTORY MUSEUM
Before Pentium processors and IPOs, there were 50-cent bonds and

gold dust. See an authentic stagecoach and learn about the Wild West and California's pioneering fortune-seekers at this Gold Rush museum.

MAP **2** A3 **9** 420 MONTGOMERY ST.
415-396-2619

YERBA BUENA CENTER FOR THE ARTS GALLERIES

Located across from SF MOMA, this thriving center hardly pales in comparison. On offer, a rotating schedule of exhibits explores various disciplines, everything from computer art to kinetic sculpture.

MAP **2** C3 **33** 701 MISSION ST.
415-978-2787

MAP 3 | NORTH BEACH/THE WATERFRONT

ART EXCHANGE

Specializing in the resale of original paintings, drawings, sculptures, and photographs, as well as limited-edition prints, this popular gallery also sells artist memorablia and has a large sculpture garden and thematic exhibits.

MAP **3** D2 **10** 645 CHESTNUT ST.
415-474-4955

DIEGO RIVERA GALLERY AT THE S.F. ART INSTITUTE

Housed in a 1926 Spanish colonial-style building, complete with courtyard fountain and bell tower, the West's oldest art school boasts an added treat for Rivera fans.

MAP **3** D1 **8** 800 CHESTNUT ST.
415-771-7020

MUSÉE MÉCANIQUE

At San Francisco's Penny Arcade, be transported back in time at any of the 200 antique, coin-operated game machines. Photos from the 1906 earthquake, Ocean Beach carnival, and Sutro Baths line the walls.

MAP **3** B2 **3** PIER 45
415-346-2000

PAUL THIEBAUD GALLERY

Paul Thiebaud serves as the West Coast dealer for his father, famed California artist Wayne Thiebaud. His gallery specializes in realist paintings and works on paper.

MAP **3** D3 **11** 718 COLUMBUS AVE.
415-434-3055

MAP 4 MARINA/COW HOLLOW/PACIFIC HEIGHTS

AFRICAN AMERICAN HISTORICAL AND CULTURAL SOCIETY

This museum and gallery (one of five at Fort Mason) showcases African American art, artifacts, and crafts, including pieces by noted local modernist Sargent Johnson.

 MAP 4 B4 **7** FORT MASON, BLDG. C
415-441-0640

EXPLORATORIUM

At this scientific wonderland, you'll lay your hands on hundreds of interactive displays (giant bubble machine, anyone?) and understand why *Scientific American* named this the finest science museum in the country.

 MAP 4 B1 **4** 3601 LYON ST.
415-397-5673

HYDE STREET PIER HISTORIC SHIPS

A three-masted tall ship and a paddlewheel ferryboat are among the historic vessels berthed at this hands-on floating museum. USS *Pampanito*, a World War II-era submarine, is docked at adjacent Pier 45.

 MAP 4 A6 **2** 2905 HYDE ST. PIER
415-447-5000

MARITIME MUSEUM

This fine collection of maritime artifacts includes portions of Gold Rush-era ships unearthed during construction of the Transamerica Pyramid, and more than 100 sea chantey recordings.

 MAP 4 B5 **13** 900 BEACH ST.
415-447-5000

MEXICAN MUSEUM

Specializing in Mexican and Mexican American folk and fine art, this impressive museum, part of the Yerba Buena expansion project, will reopen its doors – bigger and better – in late 2006.

 MAP 4 B4 **9** FORT MASON, BLDG. D
415-202-9700

MUSEO ITALOAMERICANO

Originally located in its rightful cultural homeland of North Beach, this transplanted museum devotes itself to uncovering the arts and culture of Italians and Italian Americans.

 MAP 4 B4 **8** FORT MASON, BLDG. C
415-673-2200

MUSEUM OF CRAFT AND FOLK ART

Folk arts and crafts, from vintage Japanese kimonos to iron gates by California metalworkers, are displayed here in revolving exhibits. Many items can even be purchased.

 MAP 4 B4 **11** FORT MASON, BLDG. A
415-775-0991

EXPLORATORIUM   ASIAN ART MUSEUM

MAP 5 CIVIC CENTER/HAYES VALLEY

ASIAN ART MUSEUM
The new Asian was redesigned by Italian architect Gae Aulenti in
2003; the new building, which is housed in the San Francisco main
library, accomodates some 15,000 pieces – including jades, textiles,
and bronzes – and represents 6,000 years of Asian culture.

MAP 5 C6 ▲ 18   200 LARKIN ST.
415-581-3500

BUCHEON GALLERY
Bucheon primarily spotlights emerging artists and offers guidance
to novice buyers looking to start a collection.

MAP 5 D4 ▲ 28   389 GROVE ST.
415-863-2891

POLANCO
Specializing in Mexican arts and crafts, including woodcuts, folk art
and jewelry, and vintage fine art, this colorful gallery is a favorite of
serious collectors and designers.

MAP 5 D4 ▲ 40   393 HAYES ST.
415-252-5753

SAN FRANCISCO ARTS COMMISSION
This city-run gallery spotlights emerging national and local artists, as well as presenting periodic lectures. Down the street at the
SFAC's Grove Street Windows, you can watch video projections,
sound works, and other site-specific installations.

MAP 5 D5 ▲ 41   401 VAN NESS AVE.
415-554-6080

SAN FRANCISCO MAIN LIBRARY
At this seven-story gem of beaux arts–inspired architecture, you'll
find a five-story skylit atrium, multiple galleries, book-art exhibits,
and the San Francisco History Center.

MAP 5 D6 ▲ 50   100 LARKIN ST.
415-557-4400

SAN FRANCISCO PERFORMING ARTS LIBRARY & MUSEUM

Hardcore theater buffs can while away their daylight hours at the West Coast's largest collection of costumes, recordings, photos, books, and archives related to performing arts.

MAP 5 D5 **A** 42 401 VAN NESS AVE., 4TH FL.
415-255-4800

THOMAS REYNOLDS GALLERY

Featuring works by Henry Villierme and Mark Ulriksen (a frequent New York contributor), the gallery operates on the ethos that art improves life. Its original city- and landscapes are offered at down-to-earth prices.

MAP 5 A2 **A** 1 2291 PINE ST.
415-441-4093

MAP 6 | MISSION/CASTRO/NOE VALLEY

BLUE ROOM GALLERY

This lofted gallery has brought a splash of sophistication to the Mission's gallery scene. With its focus on interdisciplinary work, emerging artists, and gallery programs, Blue Room might make you forget you're on Mission Street.

MAP 6 C4 **A** 44 2331 MISSION ST.
415-282-8411

CELLSPACE

This popular Mission art space – officially known as the Collectively Explorative Learning Labs – is home to countless local artists and non-profits. Don't miss the monthly exhibits in its Crucible Steel Gallery.

MAP 6 C6 **A** 47 2050 BRYANT ST.
415-648-7562

ENCANTADA GALLERY

Encantada and its offshoot, Arte Popular, dispense pop culture artifacts, like the must-have Frida Kahlo tote bag, as well as nicely priced Mexican folk art.

MAP 6 C4 **A** 42 908 VALENCIA ST.
415-642-3939

GALERÍA DE LA RAZA

Since 1970, this tiny storefront gallery in the heart of the Mission district has celebrated contemporary Mexican-American culture with bimonthly shows focusing on Bay Area, Mexican, and international artists.

MAP 6 E6 **A** 67 2857 24TH ST.
415-826-8009

INTERSECTION FOR THE ARTS

At the heart of the Mission's new arts community, this venerable institution hosts solo and group exhibitions and, true to its

---

PUBLIC ART

Often fanciful in appearance and political in message, freely accessible public murals are utterly San Franciscan. Over 600 murals are scattered around the city, including fine examples from the 1930s at **Coit Tower (p. 8)**, **San Francisco Art Institute (p. 75)** and the **Beach Chalet Brewery (p. 52)**. Hundreds of murals are concentrated in the Mission district: **Balmy Alley (p. 16)** and Clarion Alley (btwn. 16th and 17th Sts.) are veritable open-air galleries teeming with the works of community muralists. For guided walking tours of Mission murals, contact **Precita Eyes Mural Arts & Visitors Center (p. 79)**.

---

name, acts as a center for the city's best performance art, theater, and dance.

 B4 ⓐ 13   446 VALENCIA ST.
415-626-2787

PRECITA EYES MURAL ARTS & VISITORS CENTER
Precita Eyes is responsible for many of the murals found within the Mission. Take one of the weekend guided walking tours of Balmy Alley and other stunning examples of Diego Rivera–inspired murals.

 E6 ⓐ 66   2981 24TH ST.
415-285-2287

 THE HAIGHT/INNER SUNSET/INNER RICHMOND

DE YOUNG MUSEUM
The new de Young, designed by Swiss architectural firm Herzog & de Meuron, aims to awe when it opens in 2005. The copper-clad structure will house the area's largest and most diverse collection of art from the Americas, the Pacific Islands, and Africa.

MAP 7 D2 ⓐ 12   75 TEA GARDEN DR.
415-750-3600

 GOLDEN GATE PARK

PALACE OF THE LEGION OF HONOR
See SIGHTS, p. 18

MAP 8 A3 ⓞ 2   100 34TH AVE.
415-863-3330

PERFORMING ARTS

MAP 1 | UNION SQUARE

AMERICAN CONSERVATORY THEATER (ACT)/ GEARY THEATER *THEATER*
Considered one of the nation's best theater companies (alums include Oscar winner Denzel Washington and Annette Bening), ACT brings revivals and premieres to the landmark elegance of the Geary Theater.

MAP 1 D3❹44 415 GEARY ST.
415-749-2228 (ACT), 415-834-3200 (GEARY THEATER)

CONCERTS AT GRACE CATHEDRAL *MUSIC VENUE*
Perched atop Nob Hill, this world-famous cathedral hosts regular musical recitals and lectures in an ornate French-gothic setting. Due to donations from supporters, most of the organ recitals are free to the public.

MAP 1 B1❹4 1100 CALIFORNIA ST.
415-749-6355

CURRAN THEATRE *THEATER*
Spotlighting current Broadway musicals and dramas (the theater's most famous run was of Andrew Lloyd Webber's *Phantom of the Opera*), the Curran also showcases experimental works such as the Pulitzer Prize–winning *Topdog/Underdog*.

MAP 1 D2❹40 445 GEARY ST.
415-551-2000

SAN FRANCISCO PERFORMANCES *VARIOUS*
This nonprofit organization presents dance, chamber music, vocal recitals, and jazz in various venues around the city, and also commissions new works. Call for a schedule of performances.

MAP 1 C3❹17 500 SUTTER ST., STE. 710
415-398-6449

POST STREET THEATRE *THEATER*
Incongruously located within the Kensington Park Hotel, this space served as an Elks Club auditorium before being converted into a theater in 1982. The theater presents a variety of Off-Broadway and avant-garde productions.

MAP 1 D3❹41 450 POST ST. (KENSINGTON PARK HOTEL)
415-321-2900

MAP 2 CHINATOWN/FINANCIAL DISTRICT/SOMA

GOLDEN GATE THEATRE *THEATER*
A first-run movie house and vaudeville stage in the 1920s, this theater now presents the best of Broadway musicals. *Mamma Mia* was showcased here as part of the Best of Broadway series.

 D2 **A42** 1 TAYLOR ST.
415-551-2000

LINES BALLET *DANCE COMPANY*
Contemporary dancer Alonzo King leads this touring company and operates the largest dance center outside of New York. Call for a schedule of classes and local performances.

 D2 **A43** 26 7TH ST.
415-863-3040

METREON *ENTERTAINMENT CENTER*
With nine restaurants and 16 movie screens (one of them a giant IMAX) to choose from, dinner and a movie has never been easier than at Sony's first "urban entertainment center."

 C3 **A31** 101 4TH ST.
800-638-7366

YERBA BUENA CENTER FOR THE ARTS THEATER *THEATER*
With its striking blue facade, this architecturally significant theater hosts a well-respected yearly program of theatrical and musical performances featuring the city's top artists, dance companies, and musicians.

 C3 **A34** 700 HOWARD ST.
415-978-2787

 MAP 4 MARINA/COW HOLLOW/PACIFIC HEIGHTS

BATS IMPROV *THEATER*
The art of improvisation is a competitive sport at the Bayfront Theater. Watch the actors sparring, or take a class.

 B4 **A6** FORT MASON, BLDG. B
415-474-8935

CLAY THEATRE *THEATER*
Originally a nickelodeon movie house, this art deco theater shows first-run international and independent films.

 E3 **A53** 2261 FILLMORE ST.
415-267-4893

LUMIERE *THEATER*
This tucked-away theater caters to the nocturnal theater crowd and specializes in avant-garde and international films.

E6 **A57** 1572 CALIFORNIA ST.
415-267-4893

MAGIC THEATRE *THEATER*
This important venue gave birth to Sam Shepard's career with *La Turista* in 1971. The theater continues to host world-premieres.

 MAP 4 B4 Ⓐ10   FORT MASON, BLDG. D
415-441-8822

OLD FIRST CONCERTS *MUSIC VENUE*
This serene, Romanesque, wood-beamed church makes a beautiful setting for its year-round series of choral, jazz, and chamber music recitals, with performances from Bay Area musicians and other highly acclaimed performers.

 MAP 4 E6 Ⓐ56   1751 SACRAMENTO ST.
415-474-1608

PALACE OF FINE ARTS THEATRE *THEATER*
This theater, set near the Palace's classical columns and reflecting pools, showcases everything from children's musicals to film retrospectives.

 MAP 4 C1 Ⓐ21   3301 LYON ST.
415-563-6504

MAP 5 CIVIC CENTER/HAYES VALLEY

THE CENTER *VARIOUS*
This bold LGBT center offers a little bit of everything for the queer community. On any given evening, you'll find poetry readings, plays, and visual art exhibits under way.

 MAP 5 F4 Ⓐ66   1800 MARKET ST.
415- 865-5555

CITY ARTS & LECTURES *VARIOUS*
High-profile writers and artists discuss their works, usually at the plush Herbst Theatre. The conversations are recorded for broadcast on National Public Radio.

 MAP 5 D5 Ⓐ43   401 VAN NESS AVE.
415-392-4400

THE FILLMORE *MUSIC VENUE*
Opened in the late 1960s, the Fillmore ignited the careers of legendary bands such as Santana and The Grateful Dead. This popular venue now hosts everything from concerts to theme parties.

 MAP 5 B2 Ⓐ9   1805 GEARY BLVD.
415-346-6000

GREAT AMERICAN MUSIC HALL *MUSIC VENUE*
Consistently voted one of the best places to hear live music, this premier concert venue stays true to its name, staging nightly shows by greats, such as the Rolling Stones, to sold-out crowds.

MAP 5 B5 Ⓐ14   859 O'FARRELL ST.
415-885-0750

HERBST THEATRE *THEATER*
This elegant theater was the site of the U.N. Charter signing in 1945,

DAVIES SYMPHONY HALL   WAR MEMORIAL OPERA HOUSE

and now hosts an endless array of concerts, screenings, and the ever-popular City Arts & Lectures series.

MAP **5** D5 **Ⓐ44**   401 VAN NESS AVE.
415-392-4400

NEW CONSERVATORY THEATRE CENTER (NCTC) *THEATER*
A performing-arts complex, NCTC stages Gay Pride Season dramas and comedies, and also runs youth educational programs, an art gallery, and a video studio.

MAP **5** E5 **Ⓐ56**   25 VAN NESS AVE.
415-861-8972

ORPHEUM THEATRE *THEATER*
The Orpheum is *the* venue to catch top-notch Broadway musicals and plays. Recent classics, such as *Rent* and *The Lion King,* debuted at this 2,200-seat house.

MAP **5** D6 **Ⓐ51**   1192 MARKET ST.
415-551-2000

PHILHARMONIA BAROQUE ORCHESTRA *CLASSICAL MUSIC GROUP*
Music director Nicholas McGegan leads most of the 40 Bay Area concerts a year. The orchestra is dedicated to performing historically informed pieces on medieval European instruments.

MAP **5** C5 **Ⓐ17**   180 REDWOOD ST.
415-252-1288

SAN FRANCISCO BALLET *BALLET COMPANY*
The oldest ballet company in the nation resides at the War Memorial Opera House and launched a national holiday tradition when it staged the U.S. premiere of the *Nutcracker* in 1944.

MAP **5** D4 **Ⓐ25**   455 FRANKLIN ST.
415-865-2000

SAN FRANCISCO OPERA *OPERA COMPANY*
Founded in 1923, San Francisco Opera presents classics and new, commissioned works at the beaux arts–style War Memorial Opera House. Performances are in original languages with English supertitles.

MAP **5** D5 **Ⓐ45**   301 VAN NESS AVE.
415-864-3330

SAN FRANCISCO SYMPHONY/
DAVIES SYMPHONY HALL   *MUSIC VENUE*

Acoustically renovated in 1992, Davies Symphony Hall is home to
Michael Tilson Thomas's San Francisco Symphony. The symphony's
free performance of Beethoven's Ninth in Golden Gate Park after the
1989 quake won the hearts of San Franciscans.

 D5 **48**   201 VAN NESS AVE.
415-864-6000

WAR MEMORIAL OPERA HOUSE   *MUSIC VENUE*

This beaux arts–style building, designed by Coit Tower and City Hall
architect Arthur Brown, Jr., houses the San Francisco Opera and San
Francisco Ballet. Tours are available Mondays between 10 A.M. and 2 P.M.

 D5 **46**   301 VAN NESS AVE.
415-865-2000

WOMEN'S PHILHARMONIC   *CLASSICAL MUSIC GROUP*

Since 1981 this all-women orchestra has featured new and commissioned works by 150 female composers. They've garnered numerous
awards and have created various educational programs.

 E5 **57**   44 PAGE ST., STE. 604D
415-437-0123

MAP 6 | MISSION/CASTRO/NOE VALLEY

BRAVA!   *THEATER*

This grassroots theater serves up strong artistic takes on multicul-
turalism, lesbianism, and feminism. With a focus on the creation of
new work, it showcases plays by women of color and lesbians.

 E6 **68**   2781 24TH ST.
415-641-7657

CASTRO THEATRE   *THEATER*

Opened in 1922, this historic landmark adds pomp and pageantry to
the movie-going experience. A Mighty Wurlitzer pipe organ opens
most film-festival and premiere screenings.

 C2 **29**   429 CASTRO ST.
415-621-6120

THE MARSH   *THEATER*

Stirring up the Mission's socio-cultural melting pot, local actors,
dancers, and comedians perform 500 shows a year for audiences
that enjoy new and experimental work.

 D4 **49**   1062 VALENCIA ST.
415-641-0235

ODC THEATER   *THEATER*

Home to ODC San Francisco, an award-winning modern dance company, this space offers an eclectic performance schedule, including
contemporary dance, ethnic dance, music, and theater.

MAP 6 B5 **25**   3153 17TH ST.
415-863-9834

CASTRO THEATRE   THE ROXIE CINEMA

ROBERT MOSES' KIN *THEATER*
Acclaimed artistic director Robert Moses has produced 40 original
and provocative works since 1995. Collaborations with jazz ensembles and community groups ensures consistently dynamic seasons.

MAP 6 B5 ⚑ 26   3153 17TH ST.
415-252-8384

THE ROXIE CINEMA *THEATER*
This Mission classic features new and controversial films and isn't
afraid to take risks, especially with its lowest-in-town candy prices.
Pick up a catalog so as not to miss the exceptional programming.

MAP 6 B4 ⚑ 18   3117 16TH ST.
415-863-1087

THEATRE RHINOCEROS *THEATER*
The longest-running queer theater company in the nation presents
cutting-edge productions on its Mission-district stage. The Thursdays
and Fridays prior to opening nights are "pay what you can nights."

MAP 6 B5 ⚑ 23   2926 16TH ST.
415-861-5079

A TRAVELING JEWISH THEATRE *THEATER*
One of the first acting ensembles to tour Eastern Europe after
the Cold War stages original productions in a space at the Project
Artaud performing arts complex.

MAP 6 B6 ⚑ 27   470 FLORIDA ST.
415-399-1809

MAP 7 | THE HAIGHT/INNER SUNSET/INNER RICHMOND

RED VIC *THEATER*
This little movie house knows the true meaning of independent, with
its seating converted from church pews and couches, art-house film
schedule, and organic refreshments. Only in San Francisco!

MAP 7 E4 ⚑ 29   1727 HAIGHT ST.
415-668-3994

RECREATION

 CHINATOWN/FINANCIAL DISTRICT/SOMA

BARBARY COAST TRAIL
Follow bronze sidewalk plaques to 20 historic sights and recall San Francisco's hedonistic past – from Asian temples to the historic ships at Aquatic Park – on this 3.8-mile self-guided tour.

 D3 ⓐ 47   START AT OLD MINT, 5TH AND MISSION STS.
415-775-1111

THE EMBARCADERO
Walk, run, cycle, or in-line skate your way along the San Francisco waterfront, all the way from South Beach to Pier 23. Stop at the Ferry Building for a break and a tasty snack.

 D5 ⓐ 62   START AT 2ND AND KING STS.

JUSTIN HERMAN PLAZA
When the weather's nice, this downtown plaza near the waterfront is a popular brown-bag lunch spot. During the holiday season, though, it becomes a festive outdoor skating rink.

 A4 ⓐ 11   MARKET ST. AT EMBARCADERO

YERBA BUENA GARDENS
See SIGHTS, p. 5.

 C3 ✪ 32   3RD ST. BTWN. MISSION AND FOLSOM STS.
415-543-1718 (ARTS AND EVENTS INFORMATION)

 NORTH BEACH/THE WATERFRONT

BAY CRUISES
These one-hour cruises are packed with photo ops: San Francisco from the bay, the Golden Gate Bridge before passing underneath, and Alcatraz up close and personal.

B3 ⓐ 5   BLUE AND GOLD FLEET: PIER 39
415-773-1188

GREENWICH STEPS
Ferns, vines, and conifers line this brick staircase leading up to Coit

WASHINGTON SQUARE   JAPANESE TEA GARDEN

Tower. It takes some effort, but you'll reap fantastic views of the sky-line, bay, and bridges.

 MAP 3 D5 **Ⓐ16** GREENWICH ST. BTWN. SANSOME ST. AND TELEGRAPH HILL BLVD.

WASHINGTON SQUARE
This patch of green sits in the heart of Italian North Beach. Join the morning tai chi exercises or check out the 1879 statue of Benjamin Franklin.

 MAP 3 D3 **Ⓐ12** FILBERT ST. AT STOCKTON ST.

MAP 4 | MARINA/COW HOLLOW/PACIFIC HEIGHTS

AQUATIC PARK
This sheltered beach serves as the base for many waterfront events, from July Fourth fireworks to impromptu street performances. Stroll its length or sit and enjoy the views.

 MAP 4 A5 **Ⓐ1** POLK ST. AT BEACH ST.

CITY GUIDES FREE WALKING TOURS: ART DECO MARINA
This volunteer-guided tour showcases the Marina district's impressive art deco architecture. The tours take place on the second Sunday of the month at 11 A.M. Call for details on tours of other neighborhoods.

 MAP 4 C4 **Ⓐ26** MEET AT 1890 CHESTNUT ST. (MARINA LIBRARY) 415-557-4266

CRISSY FIELD
Stretching to the foot of the Golden Gate Bridge, Crissy Field is great for running, biking, in-line skating, fishing, bird-watching, or just sleeping on the shoreline.

 MAP 4 B1 **Ⓐ3** NORTH OF MASON ST. BTWN. PALACE OF FINE ARTS AND FORT POINT 415-427-4779

MARINA GREEN
Perfect for flying kites, this bayside field is also a favorite for

naps, jogs, and picnics. Grab a bite from any of the restaurants on Chestnut Street and enjoy the panoramic views.

 B3 **A5** MARINA BLVD. AT FILLMORE ST.

MAP 6 | MISSION/CASTRO/NOE VALLEY

CORONA HEIGHTS
A moderate uphill stroll from the Castro leads to this bare, rocky open space with lovely views of downtown and the San Francisco Bay. Hike up in the evening for a dazzling California sunset.

 B1 **A6** ROOSEVELT WAY AT 15TH ST.

CRUISIN' THE CASTRO WALKING TOUR
Learn all about the Castro district, including its people, its beautiful architecture, and its fascinating, varied history, on this 4-hour walking tour (lunch included). Reservations are required.

 C1 **A28** START AT 400 CASTRO ST.
415-550-8110

DOLORES PARK
This pleasant neighborhood park welcomes family picnics, a game of soccer, dog walking, or just lounging about. The sloping, grassy space fills with sunbathers on warm days. Use caution here at night.

 C3 **A31** DOLORES ST. AT 20TH ST.

MAP 7 | THE HAIGHT/INNER SUNSET/INNER RICHMOND

BUENA VISTA PARK
A wooded hill just a short walk from the Haight-Ashbury intersection, this park offers sweeping city and bay views from the top. Do not venture here at night, though.

 E6 **A34** HAIGHT ST. AT LYON ST.

HAIGHT ASHBURY FLOWER POWER WALKING TOUR
Spend a couple of hours learning about the Haight's history, Victorian architecture, and the homes of its many famous figures. Tuesdays and Saturdays, 9:30 A.M.

 E4 **A26** START AT STANYAN ST. AT WALLER ST.
415-863-1621

JAPANESE TEA GARDEN
On a stroll through this garden, you'll encounter a moon bridge, a Zen garden, and a landmark pagoda. Afterward, enjoy some jasmine or green tea in the open-air teahouse.

 D1 **A11** HAGIWARA TEA GARDEN DR. AT MLK JR. DR.
415-752-4227

DAY TRIPS

If you have a day or even just part of one to spare, glorious recreation spots – from monumental redwoods to gorgeous Pacific shores – are within easy reach off Highway 1. A quick trip north over the Golden Gate Bridge leads to **Muir Woods,** a grove of ancient redwood trees crisscrossed by hiking paths both long and short (one's even wheelchair accessible). Some trails connect to those in the adjacent **Mt. Tamalpais State Park,** which offers unbeatable Bay Area views. Farther north is the spectacular **Point Reyes National Seashore,** where you can hike for miles, lounge on the beach, or (during winter and spring) watch elephant seals play and whales swim past the wind-whipped oceanfront cliffs.

PRESIDIO GOLF COURSE

This gorgeous but challenging 18-hole golf course winds through eucalyptus trees and Monterey pines and contains a number of those trademark San Francisco hills.

 MAP 7 A3 ● 1 300 FINLEY RD.
415-561-4653

STRYBING ARBORETUM AND BOTANICAL GARDEN

Stroll among the 55 acres of unusual trees and flowers, or sit with a book and a picnic beside a pond or fountain. Free guided walks daily at 1:30 P.M.

 MAP 7 E1 ● 22 MLK JR. DR. NEAR 9TH AVE. AND LINCOLN WAY
415-661-1316

MAP 8 GOLDEN GATE PARK

GOLDEN GATE PARK

See SIGHTS, p. 17.

 MAP 8 D4 ● 15 STANYAN AT FELL ST. (MAIN ENTRANCE), JFK DR.
(MCLAREN LODGE VISITOR CENTER) 415-831-2700

LANDS END

Short hiking trails lead from the parking lot at Sutro Baths into the woods and along the cliffs. Situated on the California Coastal Trail, Lands End accesses Lincoln Park (north) and Ocean Beach (south).

 MAP 8 B1 ● 6 START FROM WEST END OF POINT LOBOS AVE.
NEAR GREAT HIGHWAY

LINCOLN PARK

Facing the Marin Headlands, Lincoln Park offers beautiful ocean views and a series of short, easy trails. A section of the California

SUTRO HEIGHTS
PARK

BAKER BEACH

Coastal Trail connects the park with Land's End (south) and the
Presidio (north).

MAP 8 A2 🅐1   ENTER NEAR LEGION OF HONOR DR. AND EL CAMINO DEL MAR

OCEAN BEACH

A beachfront running path extends along the Great Highway, with
views of crashing waves. However, the chilly waters and strong rip-
tides here make surfing a challenge and swimming a risk.

MAP 8 D1 🅐14   GREAT HIGHWAY AT FULTON ST.

QUEEN WILHELMINA TULIP GARDENS

This small garden, with its benches, plots of tulips, and a restored
1902 Dutch windmill, is most beautiful in the spring and late summer.

MAP 8 D1 🅐12   JFK DR. AT GREAT HIGHWAY
415-831-2700

STOW LAKE/STRAWBERRY HILL

Rent a boat to paddle across Stow Lake. Then trek to the top of
Strawberry Hill for city and park views.

MAP 8 D6 🅐16   EAST OF CROSSOVER DR. BTWN. JFK AND MLK JR. DRS.
415-752-0347

SUTRO HEIGHTS PARK

This park was once the grounds of the Adolph Sutro estate. The
mansion no longer exists, but some of the walls remain. Look for
hidden statues among the trees.

MAP 8 B1 🅐8   POINT LOBOS AVE. AT 48TH AVE.
415-561-4323 (PRESIDIO VISITOR CENTER)

OVERVIEW MAP

BAKER BEACH

Baker Beach is a local favorite for its premium bridge views and long
stretch of sand. For the free-spirited, swimsuits are optional at the
northern end.

OVERVIEW MAP C2   WEST OF LINCOLN BLVD. ON GIBSON RD.

 HOTELS

Trendsetter favorite: **CLIFT,** p. 92

Funkiest decor: **PHOENIX HOTEL,** p. 98

Unique amenities: **HOTEL TRITON,** p. 93

Best views: **MANDARIN ORIENTAL,** p. 95

Best service: **CAMPTON PLACE HOTEL,** p. 92

You-only-live-once splurge:
RITZ-CARLTON SAN FRANCISCO, p. 95

Most romantic: **FOUR SEASONS,** p. 95

MAP 1 | UNION SQUARE

THE ANDREWS HOTEL   *QUAINT* $

European flair and homey touches, like down comforters, continental breakfasts on each floor, and a complimentary wine hour in the cozy lobby, put guests at ease in this Union Square hotel.

MAP 1 D2 🅗 34   624 POST ST.
415-563-6877 OR 800-926-3739

CAMPTON PLACE HOTEL   *GRAND* $$$

Behind the discreet brownstone facade is a landmark hotel famous for its exceptional service and for the understated luxury that permeates every inch, including the spacious limestone bathrooms.

MAP 1 C4 🅗 20   340 STOCKTON ST.
415-781-5555 OR 800-235-4300

CLIFT   *CHIC* $$

Designed by Ian Schrager and Philippe Starck, the Clift astounds guests with cartoonishly oversized lobby furniture, surreal sculptures, and Murano glass lamps. The cool white and beige rooms, suites, and lofts keep it classic.

MAP 1 D2 🅗 39   495 GEARY ST.
415-775-4700 OR 800-606-6090

THE COMMODORE HOTEL   *CHIC* $

The inspired luxury-liner motif (try the Titanic café for breakfast) and reasonable rates make up for smallish rooms and noisy neighbors. The funky Red Room Bar downstairs is a weekend hotspot.

MAP 1 D1 🅗 32   825 SUTTER ST.
415-923-6800 OR 800-338-6848

EXECUTIVE HOTEL VINTAGE COURT   *ROMANTIC* $$

"Vintage" refers to wine at this elegant Napa Valley–themed hotel. Share a bottle over dinner at Masa's, then retreat to the Niebaum-Coppola penthouse suite, with its wood-burning fireplace, whirlpool tub, and cityscape views.

MAP 1 B4 🅗 9   650 BUSH ST.
415-392-4666 OR 800-654-1100

THE FAIRMONT   *GRAND* $$$

A piece of San Francisco history, this Nob Hill landmark dates from 1907. Architect Julia Morgan's showpiece boasts sumptuous marble baths and, from the newer north tower, unobstructed views of the bay.

MAP 1 A2 🅗 1   950 MASON ST.
415-772-5000 OR 800-527-4727

HOTEL ADAGIO   *CHIC* $

Recently renovated, the Adagio blends Spanish colonial revival architecture and upscale urban minimalism with surprising success. Business travelers appreciate the free, in-room high-speed Internet and state-of-the-art fitness center.

MAP 1 D2 🅗 36   550 GEARY ST.
415-775-5000 OR 800-228-8830

THE ANDREWS HOTEL   HOTEL MONACO

HOTEL BIJOU *CHIC* *$*
This aptly named jewel box of a hotel celebrates 1930s film grandeur in the gritty Tenderloin. Movies with a San Francisco connection play nightly in the lobby's minitheater.

MAP 1 **F3 ⊕ 59** 111 MASON ST.
415-771-1200 OR 800-771-1022

HOTEL DIVA *CHIC* *$*
With its star-studded clientele and prime spot on Theater Row, Hotel Diva lives up to its name. The minimalist decor and Internet connections in every room attract design-savvy travelers.

MAP 1 **D2 ⊕ 37** 440 GEARY ST.
415-885-0200 OR 800-553-1900

HOTEL MONACO *CHIC* *$$*
Its stunning marble lobby and eclectic French-inspired decor help make this boutique hotel a San Francisco favorite. Canopies and striped wallpaper brighten the pet-friendly rooms.

MAP 1 **D2 ⊕ 38** 501 GEARY ST.
415-292-0100 OR 866 622-5284

HOTEL NIKKO *CHIC* *$$*
From its cool marble lobby to its richly decorated rooms, quiet refinement permeates this Japanese-owned hotel. Several suites feature rock gardens, shoji screens, and granite soaking tubs.

MAP 1 **E3 ⊕ 56** 222 MASON ST.
415-394-1111

HOTEL REX *QUAINT* *$$*
Inspired by the literary salons of 1930s San Francisco and Paris, and named for hometown Beat poet Kenneth Rexroth, this unique downtown refuge juxtaposes dataports with antique writing desks.

MAP 1 **C3 ⊕ 16** 562 SUTTER ST.
415-433-4434 OR 800-433-4434

HOTEL TRITON *CHIC* *$$*
A longtime favorite of the entertainment industry for its playfully designed rooms, the eco-friendly Triton abounds with extra touches, like Frette sheets, on-site yoga classes, and a meditation room.

MAP 1 **C5 ⊕ 22** 342 GRANT ST.
415-394-0500 OR 800-800-1299

INTERCONTINENTAL MARK   HOTEL PALOMAR
HOPKINS

THE HUNTINGTON HOTEL   *GRAND* $$$
Neighboring Grace Cathedral atop Nob Hill, this elegant grande dame has lavish rooms, one of the city's best hotel pools (overlooking Union Square), and a world-class on-site spa.

MAP 1 B2 **H** 5   1075 CALIFORNIA ST.
415-474-5400 OR 800-227-4683

INTERCONTINENTAL MARK HOPKINS   *GRAND* $$$
At this destination hotel, rooms dazzle with an eccentric interpretation of classical elements, but sweeping bay views, roof terraces, and marble-embellished hot tubs make the suites truly awe-inspiring.

MAP 1 B2 **H** 6   999 CALIFORNIA ST.
415-392-3434 OR 800-662-4455

KENSINGTON PARK HOTEL   *ROMANTIC* $
This hotel unites grand San Francisco elegance with such cosmopolitan conveniences as in-room fax machines. Located in the historic Lodge Building, the Kensington charms with old-fashioned quirks, like an antique elevator bench.

MAP 1 D3 **H** 41   450 POST ST.
415-788-6400

OMNI SAN FRANCISCO HOTEL   *GRAND* $$
This restored 1926 building retains its neo-Renaissance style while providing its guests with modern-day amenities. The 362 guest rooms, decorated with 1920s and 1930s accents, feature Chinese marble vanities and 330-count Egyptian cotton sheets.

MAP 1 A6 **H** 2   500 CALIFORNIA ST.
415-677-9494

ORCHARD HOTEL   *CHIC* $$
Whether for business or pleasure, guests come to this understated, 10-story boutique hotel to be pampered. High-thread-count sheets, cotton robes, and DVD surround systems in every room do the trick.

MAP 1 C4 **H** 19   665 BUSH ST.
415-362-8878 OR 888-717-2881

PETITE AUBERGE   *QUAINT* $
Faithful European tourists return to the "little inn" for its cozy

rooms, complete with gas fireplaces and armoires, and for the delightful breakfast nook, where wine is served every evening.

MAP 1 C2 ⓗ15 845 BUSH ST.
415-928-6000 OR 800-365-3004

RENAISSANCE STANFORD COURT *GRAND* $$
Built on the site of railroad baron Leland Stanford's mansion, the Stanford Court retains much of the grandeur of that era with its beaux arts fountain and Tiffany stained-glass dome.

MAP 1 B3 ⓗ7 905 CALIFORNIA ST.
415-989-3500

RITZ-CARLTON SAN FRANCISCO *GRAND* $$$
Housed in a 1909 neoclassical building, the luxurious Ritz is in a class by itself. This nine-story architectural landmark boasts top-notch service, sumptuous decor, and the feel of a bygone era.

MAP 1 B4 ⓗ8 600 STOCKTON ST.
415-296-7465 OR 800-241-3333

WESTIN ST. FRANCIS *GRAND* $$
Facing Union Square, this colorful San Francisco institution opened in 1904, survived the earthquake, and has been impressing world leaders and tourists alike ever since. Chic glass elevators add a modern touch.

MAP 1 D3 ⓗ43 335 POWELL ST.
415-397-7000

MAP 2 CHINATOWN/FINANCIAL DISTRICT/SOMA

FOUR SEASONS *ROMANTIC* $$$
This exclusive 36-floor hotel seduces privacy-seekers with its spacious rooms, floor-to-ceiling windows, ultrasoft beds, and luxurious bathtubs. A deluxe health club and spa sit on the ground level.

MAP 2 C3 ⓗ29 757 MARKET ST.
415-633-3000

HOTEL PALOMAR *CHIC* $$
Discreetly tucked into the top five floors of a 1908 building near Union Square, the sleek, 198-room Palomar offers the luxury of a boutique hotel with a minimalist edge.

MAP 2 C3 ⓗ28 12 4TH ST.
415-348-1111 OR 866-373-4941

MANDARIN ORIENTAL *GRAND* $$$
Atop the 48-story First Interstate building, the Mandarin provides stunning views as well as binoculars with which to better appreciate them. The approximate 1:1 staff-to-guest ratio ensures attentive service.

MAP 2 B4 ⓗ22 222 SANSOME ST.
415-276-9888 OR 800-622-0404

PALACE HOTEL *GRAND* $$$
This 1875 landmark (given a major facelift in 1991) hosted Winston

Churchill and FDR. Showstoppers include the Garden Court, with 80,000 pieces of stained glass, and the pool, the grandest in the city.

MAP 2 B3 🄗21   2 NEW MONTGOMERY ST.
415-512-1111 OR 800-325-3535

W SAN FRANCISCO   *CHIC* $$$
With its dramatic three-story lobby fashioned from metal and imported stone, the hip W is a true urban oasis. Spa robes, down comforters, and attentive 24-hour service are pampering touches.

MAP 2 C4 🄗39   181 3RD ST.
415-777-5300 OR 877-946-8357

MAP 3 | NORTH BEACH/THE WATERFRONT

HOTEL BOHÈME   *QUAINT* $
In the heart of North Beach, the Bohème was a favorite of Beat poets like Allen Ginsberg (his room was number 204). Rooms are small but charming, their ochre walls cluttered with Beat memorabilia.

MAP 3 E4 🄗24   444 COLUMBUS AVE.
415-433-9111

MAP 4 | MARINA/COW HOLLOW/PACIFIC HEIGHTS

THE ARGONAUT   *QUAINT* $$
Once a cannery warehouse, this boutique hotel blends authentic touches – exposed-brick walls, wood beams, a maritime clock in the lobby – with a playful nautical theme. Suites have sea-view hot tubs and telescopes.

MAP 4 B6 🄗14   495 JEFFERSON ST.
415-563-0800 OR 866-415-0704

HOTEL DEL SOL   *QUAINT* $
Kick back at this yellow 1950s-style motor court hotel. Take a dip in the pool, chill in the courtyard hammock, or relax in your bright, California beach house–style room.

MAP 4 C4 🄗29   3100 WEBSTER ST.
415-921-5520 OR 877-433-5765

HOTEL DRISCO   *GRAND* $$
Former-president Eisenhower was a regular at this 1903 luxury hotel. Today, celebrities and low-key travelers appreciate this Pacific Heights gem for its genteel ambience and modern amenities.

MAP 4 E2 🄗50   2901 PACIFIC AVE.
415-346-2880 OR 800-634-7277

HOTEL MAJESTIC   *ROMANTIC* $
Built as a railroad magnate's private residence in 1902, the Majestic

THE ARGONAUT   JACKSON COURT

resonates with history and elegance. Most of the lovely rooms feature claw-foot tubs and gas fireplaces.

 MAP 4 F5 **H71** 1500 SUTTER ST.
415-441-1100 OR 800-869-8966

JACKSON COURT *QUAINT* $
This private mansion turned bed-and-breakfast nestles in a quiet
Pacific Heights neighborhood. Antiques fill the spacious rooms, and
afternoon tea and cookies are served by the parlor fireplace.

 MAP 4 E4 **H54** 2198 JACKSON ST.
415-929-7670

THE QUEEN ANNE *ROMANTIC* $
Brimming with English heirlooms and fresh flowers, this four-story
Victorian is perennially popular with European tourists for its great
location. Ask for a suite with a wood-burning fireplace.

 MAP 4 F5 **H70** 1590 SUTTER ST.
415-441-2828

UNION STREET INN *ROMANTIC* $$
This small Edwardian bed-and-breakfast opened its doors more than
30 years ago and attracts honeymooners with its old-world ambience. The private carriage house has its own lush garden and double
whirlpool tub.

 MAP 4 D3 **H39** 2229 UNION ST.
415-346-0424

MAP 5 | CIVIC CENTER/HAYES VALLEY

THE ARCHBISHOP'S MANSION *ROMANTIC* $
Right on Alamo Square, this opulent 1904 French chateau was
built for the archbishop of San Francisco. The romantic Don
Giovanni suite comes with a four-poster bed, two fireplaces, and
an enormous bathtub.

 MAP 5 D2 **H20** 1000 FULTON ST.
415-563-7872 OR 800-543-5820

CHATEAU TIVOLI   *QUAINT* $

This Alamo Square Victorian bed-and-breakfast was once the private home of Ernestine Kreling, the founder of the West Coast's first opera house. Photos of opera singer Enrico Caruso and artist Lola Montez adorn the walls.

MAP 5 D2 ✪19   1057 STEINER ST.
415-776-5462 OR 800-228-1647

INN AT THE OPERA   *ROMANTIC* $$

Well-appointed rooms and proximity to the War Memorial Opera House draw cultured couples to this elegant inn. Have a pre-opera glass of champagne at Ovation, the sumptuous hotel restaurant.

MAP 5 D4 ✪24   333 FULTON ST.
415-863-8400 OR 800-590-0157

NOB HILL HOTEL   *ROMANTIC* $

For affordable romance with a gothic touch, check in to this Victorian-era hotel, one of the oldest in the city. Canopied beds, alabaster chandeliers, and seemingly endless hallways complete the period feel.

MAP 5 A6 ✪2   835 HYDE ST.
415-885-2987

PHOENIX HOTEL   *CHIC* $

Located in a rather dicey part of the Tenderloin, this longtime rock-star haunt puts a kitschy spin on its 1950s motel-style architecture. Balconies look out over a fantastic swimming pool.

MAP 5 C5 ✪15   601 EDDY ST.
415-776-1380 OR 800-248-9466

THE YORK HOTEL   *ROMANTIC* $

Famous for its cameo in Alfred Hitchcock's *Vertigo*, the York exudes old-school glamour (if unremarkable rooms). Its Plush Room — one of the best cabaret houses in the city — showcases acts like Rita Moreno.

MAP 5 A6 ✪3   940 SUTTER ST.
415-885-6800

MAP 6 MISSION/CASTRO/NOE VALLEY

INN ON CASTRO *QUAINT* $
This eight-room inn, located in a restored Edwardian house, sits in the heart of the Castro district. Exemplary breakfasts, as well as sherry, are included.

 MAP 6 B2 ⓗ 8   321 CASTRO ST.
415-861-0321

 MAP 7 THE HAIGHT/INNER SUNSET/INNER RICHMOND

RED VICTORIAN *QUAINT* $
It's always the Summer of Love at this 1904 Victorian in the Haight. Book the Flower Child room with its exuberant colors and 1960s posters adorning the walls.

 MAP 7 E4 ⓗ 30   1665 HAIGHT ST.
415-864-1978

STANYAN PARK HOTEL *QUAINT* $
This Victorian beauty (listed on the National Historic Register) resides directly across from Golden Gate Park, making it a popular choice for families and couples. Antique-filled rooms are comfortable and modern.

MAP 7 E4 ⓗ 31   750 STANYAN ST.
415-751-1000

CITY ESSENTIALS

SAN FRANCISCO AIRPORT

Several public and private transportation options are available from San Francisco International Airport (SFO), which is located 15 miles south of the city.

Bay Area Rapid Transit (BART) now connects directly with SFO's international terminal, providing a simple and relatively fast trip to downtown San Francisco (under an hour). The BART station is an easy walk or free shuttle ride from any point in the airport, and a one-way ticket to any downtown station costs $4.95.

Shuttle vans are a cost-effective transportation option for door-to-door service, though several stops may be made along the way. From the airport to downtown, the average one-way fare is $15-20 per passenger. Shuttle vans congregate on the second level of SFO above the baggage claim area. Advanced reservations guarantee a seat, but they aren't required and don't necessarily speed the process. The average cab fare to downtown is around $40.

Bay Shuttle: 415-564-3400

SFO Airporter: 650-246-8942

Supershuttle: 800-258-3826

RENTING A CAR

Most major car-rental companies are located in one central area at the airport. A free shuttle bus runs frequently between the airport terminals and the center. Several car rental agencies also have locations in or near downtown San Francisco:

Avis Rent A Car: 650-877-3156 (Airport), 415-957-9998

Hertz Rent A Car: 650-624-6600 (Airport), 415-957-9425

Thrifty Car Rental: 650-259-1313 (Airport), 415-777-2515

PARKING

With narrow streets, steep hills, and congested rush-hour traffic, driving in San Francisco can be a challenge. But that's nothing compared to the parking. While street parking is nearly impossible downtown, there are many public garages and lots throughout the city that make the process more manageable, though expensive.

PUBLIC TRANSPORTATION

Public transportation can be a time- and cost-saving alternative when navigating San Francisco. BART is a rail system that links major San Francisco neighborhoods with other Bay Area cities. BART runs from 4 A.M. until 1 A.M. on weekdays, and from 6 A.M.

and 8 A.M. until 1 A.M. on Saturdays and Sundays, respectively. BART rider guides may be picked up from any BART station. The Municipal Railway System (MUNI) traverses San Francisco via an intricate network of cable cars, trolleys, buses, streetcars, and light rail. MUNI operates primarily between 4:30 A.M. and 1 A.M., though limited Metro Owl services are available. MUNI maps may be purchased at the San Francisco Convention & Visitors Bureau's Visitor Information Center, located in Hallidie Plaza at Market and 5th Streets near Union Square. Visitors can also view and purchase MUNI maps online by logging on to www.sfmuni.com.

TAXIS

Taxis are available throughout San Francisco, though they can be scarce and difficult to hail from the street. A safer bet is to catch a taxi lined up outside the lobby of a major hotel, or to phone one ahead of time.

Black & White Checker Cab: 415-206-1900

United Cab: 415-552-8562

Yellow Cab: 415-626-2345

WEATHER

San Francisco's waterfront location means temperate weather year-round. Winters are mild, with temperatures in the 50s and snow almost unheard of. Summers are cooled by thick fog that often lingers until mid-afternoon and rolls in again at sunset. Summer temperatures can reach the 70s once the fog burns off, but typically hover in the 60s. September and October are the warmest and sunniest months; January and February are often described as the "rainy" months, though precipitation is usually light. It's critical to dress in layers in San Francisco, as temperatures can vary during a single day and from neighborhood to neighborhood.

HOURS

San Francisco is not a late-night city. Most restaurants shut their doors by midnight, while bars and lounges close by 2 A.M. BART stops running at 1 A.M., and MUNI shifts to a limited Metro Owl service after 1 A.M.

FESTIVALS AND EVENTS

JANUARY/FEBRUARY

Chinese New Year Parade and Celebration: Chinatown celebrates the lunar new year with costumed dancers, floats, and firecrackers. Early February. (Chinatown, 415-391-9680, www. chineseparade.com)

MARCH

St. Patrick's Day Parade: Don your shamrock green for this lively procession up Market Street. The Sunday before March 17. (Start at 2nd and Market Sts., 415-675-9885, www.sfstpatricks-dayparade.com)

APRIL

Cherry Blossom Festival: Japantown's rite of spring, with traditional flower arranging, tea ceremonies, and martial arts demos. Two weekends in April. (Japantown, 415-563-2313)

MAY

Cinco de Mayo: Folkloric dancing, food, mariachis, and live bands playing salsa to soca. The Sunday before May 5. (Civic Center)

Bay to Breakers Race: Join rowdy, costumed revelers for this 12K run/walk/stumble across the city. Sunday in mid-May. (Starts at Embarcadero, 415-359-2800, www.baytobreakers.com)

Carnaval: A hometown favorite, with drumming, dancing, and boisterous merry-making. The Sunday of Memorial Day weekend. (Mission District, 415-920-0125, www.carnavalsf.com)

JUNE

North Beach Festival: *Mangia!* Food booths abound at this long-running neighborhood fair. Weekend in June. (Washington Square Park and 1200-1500 blocks of Grant Ave., www.sfnorth beach.org/festival/)

San Francisco LGBT Pride Parade and Celebration: Hundreds of thousands take to the streets for this quintessentially San Franciscan party-cum-social-justice-movement. Weekend in late June. (Parade: Market St., Events: citywide, 415-864-3733, www .sfpride.org)

JULY

Fillmore Street Jazz Festival: Live performances feature known names, up-and-comers, and all that jazz. Weekend in early July. (Fillmore St. btwn. Jackson and Eddy Sts., www .fillmorejazzfestival.com)

AUGUST

Stern Grove Festival: Summer Sundays bring droves of picnickers to this free performing arts series. Sundays, June through August. (Sigmund Stern Grove at 19th Ave. and Sloat Blvd., www.sterngrove.org)

SEPTEMBER

San Francisco Blues Festival: Take in bay views and blues at this outdoor music festival, going strong since 1973. Weekend in late September. (Fort Mason, 415-979-5588, www.sfblues.com)

OCTOBER

Fleet Week: This sailor salute includes the Blue Angels' air show, Navy and Marine band performances, and the Parade of Ships. Columbus Day Weekend, early October. (Fisherman's Wharf, www.fleetweek.com/sf)

Halloween in the Castro: Get freaky and join the costumed crowds at this anything-goes street party. October 31. (Market and Castro Sts.)

NOVEMBER

Dia de Los Muertos: A hauntingly beautiful procession, replete with candlelight and dancing skeletons. November 2. (Mission district, www.dayofthedeadsf.org)

DISABLED ACCESS

BART and MUNI stations are fully accessible via street-to-concourse and street-to-platform elevators, and braille signs assist passengers with vision-impairment. Subsidized door-to-door van and taxi services cater to ADA-certified individuals who are unable to utilize certain MUNI bus and light-rail services. Handicapped parking is available throughout the city, and all public buildings have been newly constructed or retrofitted to comfortably accommodate individuals with disabilities.

SAFETY

As in any city, visitors to San Francisco should travel smart, stay alert, and take precautionary safety measures. Parts of Civic Center, South of Market (around 6th St.), and the Tenderloin (an area west of Union Square and east of Van Ness) should be avoided at night.

HEALTH AND EMERGENCY SERVICES

For immediate emergency medical service, dial 911. If urgent medical care is required without the assistance of an ambulance, the following medical centers offer 24-hour emergency care:

CALIFORNIA PACIFIC MEDICAL CENTER
MAP 4 B4   2333 BUCHANAN ST.
            415-600-3333

CALIFORNIA PACIFIC MEDICAL CENTER DAVIES CAMPUS
MAP 6 A1   CASTRO AND DUBOCE STS.
            415-565-6060

SAN FRANCISCO GENERAL HOSPITAL
OVERVIEW MAP E5   1001 POTRERO AVE.
                   415-206-8000

ST. MARY'S MEDICAL CENTER
MAP 6 C4   450 STANYAN ST.
            415-750-5700

PHARMACIES

RELIABLE REXALL
MAP 7 E4   801 IRVING ST.
            415-421-1895

RITE AID

MAP 5 E5   1496 MARKET ST.
415-626-9972

WALGREENS

MAP 6 C1   498 CASTRO ST.
415-861-3136

MEDIA AND COMMUNICATIONS

San Francisco has two daily newspapers, *San Francisco Chronicle* and *San Francisco Examiner*. The city's free weeklies, *The Bay Guardian* and *SF Weekly*, provide information about entertainment and nightlife.

Public pay phones are readily available throughout the city. Local calls cost $.50. Since long distance fees vary dramatically, calling cards are recommended.

For post office locations, call the United States Postal Service Hotline at 800-275-8777.

While many hotels offer some form of Internet access, Internet cafés are also a way to stay connected.

CAFÉ.COM

MAP 1 F3   120 MASON ST.
415-433-4001

QUETZAL INTERNET CAFÉ

MAP 4 F6   1234 POLK ST.
415-673-4181

SMOKING

Smoking is prohibited in all bars, clubs, and restaurants in California.

TIPPING

While gratuities vary based on the level of service, here are some general tipping guidelines: dinner, 15–20 percent of entire bill; porters, $2 per bag; skycaps, $2 per bag; taxi drivers, 10–15 percent of entire fare; limousines, 15–20 percent of entire fare; and valets, $2 per car.

DRY CLEANERS

GOLDEN GATE CLEANERS

MAP 3 F6   210 WASHINGTON ST.
415-397-8494

MARINA CLEANERS

MAP 4 C5   2875 VAN NESS AVE.
415-673-4219

ONE MARKET CLEANERS

MAP 2 A5   1 MARKET PLAZA
415-495-0711

PARAGON CLEANERS

MAP 1 B4   635 BUSH ST.
415-781-2646

STREET INDEX

INDEX

RESTAURANTS INDEX

NIGHTLIFE INDEX

SHOPS INDEX

HOTELS INDEX

PHOTO CREDITS

CONTRIBUTORS TO THE SECOND EDITION

ERIN CULLERTON   *Shops, Museums and Galleries, Performing Arts*
Erin Cullerton is a freelance arts and culture writer based in San Francisco. Her writing on visual arts, design, shopping, and culture has appeared in *Time Out San Francisco, ARTnews, ReadyMade, Surface, Time Out London,* and *Wired.*

RACHEL LEVIN   *Restaurants*
Rachel Levin is a San Francisco-based freelance writer who focuses on food, travel, and the outdoors. She eats out regularly for *San Francisco* magazine, and has contributed to a variety of other publications.

AMY WEAVER   *Sights, Hotels, City Essentials*
Researching San Francisco's sights and hotels for *Moon Metro San Francisco* and *Time Out San Francisco* has given Amy Weaver a tourist's appreciation for her adopted city. A former staff editor at *Travel & Leisure* magazine, she has also written about New York City for the Michelin Green Guides and about the Bay Area for *Out Traveler* and *Country Living* magazine.

KURT WOLFF   *Nightlife, Recreation*
A San Francisco resident for nearly two decades, Kurt Wolff writes about music, bars, and travel for numerous publications. He's the author of *The Rough Guide to Country Music,* among other titles, and also edits Zagat Survey's annual San Francisco nightlife guide.

OTHER CONTRIBUTORS
Ellie Behrstock, Grace Fujimoto (A Day in S.F.), Jeremy Russell, Erin Van Rheenen (Introduction, Neighborhoods)

CONTRIBUTORS TO THE FIRST EDITION
Charlie Amter, Jennifer Benson, John Lyons-Gould, Keith Rockmael, Erin Van Rheenen, Dana Weismann

MOON METRO SAN FRANCISCO
SECOND EDITION

Avalon Travel Publishing,
An Imprint of Avalon Publishing Group, Inc.

AVALON

Text and maps © 2005 by Avalon Travel Publishing
All rights reserved.

BART system map courtesy of BART.

ISBN: 1-56691-661-5
ISSN: 1537-9469

Editor: Erin Raber
Series Manager: Grace Fujimoto
Design: Jacob Goolkasian
Map Design: Mike Morgenfeld
Copy Editor: Kim Marks
Production Coordinator: Jacob Goolkasian
Graphics Coordinator: Deb Dutcher
Cartographer: Suzanne Service
Map Editor: Kat Smith
Proofreader: Kate McKinley
Indexers: Kevin Anglin, Suzanne Service
Fact Checkers: Dan Greenman, Matt Palmquist
Front cover photos: Yellow street car, © Randy Wells; Golden Gate Bridge,
© Getty Images/Royalty Free

Printed in China through Colorcraft Ltd., Hong Kong
Printing History
1st edition – 2002
2nd edition – May 2005
5 4 3 2 1

Please send all feedback about this book to:
Moon Metro San Francsico
Avalon Travel Publishing
1400 65th Street, Suite 250, Emeryville, CA 94608, USA
email: atpfeedback@avalonpub.com
website: www.moon.com

MOON METRO

- AMSTERDAM
- BARCELONA
- BERLIN
- BOSTON
- CHICAGO
- LAS VEGAS
- LONDON
- LOS ANGELES
- MIAMI
- MONTRÉAL
- NEW YORK CITY
- PARIS
- ROME
- SAN FRANCISCO
- SEATTLE
- TORONTO
- VANCOUVER
- WASHINGTON D.C.

**AVAILABLE AT YOUR FAVORITE
BOOK AND TRAVEL STORES**

www.moon.com

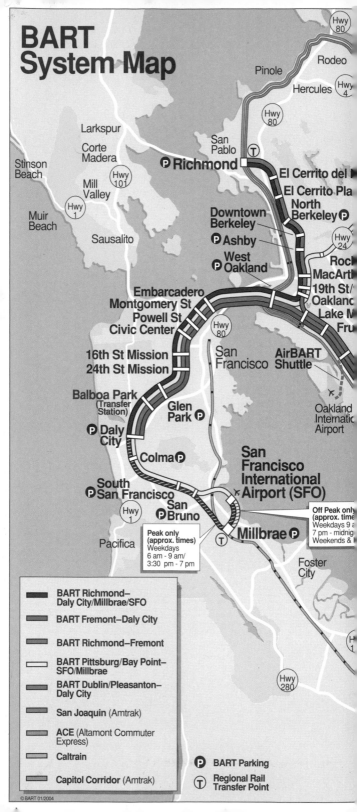